Implementing Effective Teacher Feedback Programs

The Pirozzo Process

RALPH PIROZZO

© 2024 Ralph Pirozzo

Terms of use for this publication

This work is copyright. Apart from fair dealings for the purposes of private study, research, criticism or review, or as permitted under the Copyright Act 1968 (Cth), no part should be reproduced, transmitted, stored, communicated or recorded, in any form or by any means, without the prior written permission of the copyright owner. Any enquiries regarding copyright or permissions must be made to the publisher.

You may be entitled to reproduce or communicate from this publication for educational purposes under Part VB of the Copyright Act, or for government purposes under Part VII Division 2 of the Copyright Act 1968, on the following conditions:

1. You are the purchaser, or the employee of the purchaser, of this publication, and
2. Each copy is used solely for your teaching purposes

Except as permitted by the copyright law applicable to you, you may not reproduce or communicate any CD, DVD or downloadable content purchased with this work without the prior written permission of the copyright owner.

The reproducible pages in this book are available to download at www.ambapress.com.au or www.pli.com.au

Published in 2024 by Amba Press, Melbourne, Australia.
www.ambapress.com.au

Previously published in 2015 by Hawker Brownlow Education.
This edition replaces all previous editions.

ISBN: 9781923215047 (pbk)
ISBN: 9781923215054 (ebk)

A catalogue record for this book is available from the National Library of Australia.

Contents

Introduction 1

Step 1: Find your philosophy of leadership 5

Step 2: Create a Time Allocation Inventory 13

Step 3: Build knowledge of unit planning 19

Step 4: Learn to use a variety of thinking tools 27

Step 5: Develop conflict-resolution skills 35

Step 6: Launch an effective teacher feedback program 45

Step 7: Apply four strategies for providing effective feedback 53

References 76

Acknowledgements 76

Introduction

Providing effective feedback to teachers is critical in improving teaching standards and student performance – but how can we deliver this feedback in a way that does not lead to misunderstanding, animosity or the undermining of teachers' professionalism?

In this book, I outline how schools can develop a sustainable, low-cost teacher feedback program that can be implemented in any school. I call this approach the Pirozzo Process (Figure 1, p. 2), and each chapter of the book is dedicated to one of its seven steps:

1. Find your philosophy of leadership (pp. 5–11).

    In Step 1, leaders establish a cohesive, evidence-based approach to leadership that underpins the way in which feedback is delivered.

2. Create a Time Allocation Inventory (pp. 13–17).

    By utilising the Time Allocation Inventory provided in Step 2, leaders determine exactly how much time they can commit to the feedback process.

3. Build knowledge of unit planning (pp. 19–25).

    Step 3 asks leaders to strengthen their understanding of lesson planning using the Pirozzo Matrix, an ingenious resource that cross-references Bloom's taxonomy with Gardner's multiple intelligences.

4. Learn to use a variety of thinking tools (pp. 27–34).

    Step 4 introduces leaders to a range of thinking tools that will enable them to provide clear, easy-to-understand feedback using a mutually-agreed model.

5. Develop conflict-resolution skills (pp. 35–43).

    Leaders are encouraged to familiarise themselves with research-based strategies designed to mitigate conflict that arises from the feedback process.

6. Launch an effective teacher feedback program (pp. 45–51).

    In Step 6, leaders put what they have learnt into action using Roger's diffusion of innovation theory and Lewin's (1943) force field analysis.

7. Apply four strategies for providing effective feedback (pp. 53–75).

    Step 7 offers four essential strategies for the provision of feedback: the former Sunshine Coast Region's coaching model, a unit evaluation form, classroom observation matrices and a teacher feedback form.

In implementing the Pirozzo Process, the responsibility for maintaining the efficacy of feedback rests primarily on the individual providing the feedback, referred to here as the *observer*. As the person responsible for delivering productive feedback that guides teacher

Figure 1

practice, the observer takes a leadership role. In practice, the observer could hold any of the following positions:

- principal
- deputy principal
- assistant principal
- head of department
- head of curriculum
- coach
- mentor
- peer

But regardless of their job description, an effective observer will possess the following knowledge and skills:

- excellent leadership style and outstanding time-management skills
- in-depth knowledge of unit planning
- expertise in using a variety of thinking tools
- elaborate conflict resolution skills
- capacity to implement an effective feedback program across the school
- ability to choose from four different strategies that can be used to provide feedback

It is critical to the success of the program that if the nominated observers cannot demonstrate these skills, then the Pirozzo Process should not be implemented until they have acquired these prerequisites.

In addition to the observer, the other principal participant in the feedback process is the person who receives the feedback, here referred to as the *teacher*. This is because in practice, most recipients of feedback will indeed be teachers, although the process explored in *Implementing an Effective Teacher Feedback Program* is equally applicable when providing feedback to other support staff.

Step 1
Find your philosophy of leadership

It is impossible to establish a program for effective feedback without first clarifying the leadership philosophy that underpins the process. To assist leaders in tailoring their own approaches, I have summarised five of the most influential theories of leadership:

- Kurt Lewin's three leadership styles
- Steven Covey's seven habits of highly effective people
- *The Effective Executive* by Peter F Drucker
- Michael Fullan's six secrets of change
- *Shackleton's Way* by Margot Morrell and Stephanie Capparell

In reviewing the above works, leadership emerges as a complex, challenging and multifaceted role. It also becomes clear that a leader's feedback greatly influences the people that receive it in terms of the quality of teaching and learning as well as students' learning outcomes.

Lewin's three leadership styles

Lewin is widely regarded as the founder of social psychology. In 1939, he and his associates set out to research different styles of leadership by assigning schoolchildren to one of three groups (Lewin, Uppit & White 1939). The first group was led by an *autocratic* leader; the second was led by a *democratic* leader; and the third was led by a *laissez-faire* leader. While the children participated in an arts and crafts project, the researchers observed the children's behaviour in response to the three different styles of leadership.

This groundbreaking early study was very influential in establishing three primary leadership styles:

1. Autocratic leadership

    Lewin claims that an autocratic leader

    - has clear expectations about what needs to be done, when it should be done and how it should be done
    - creates a distinction between the leader and the rest of the group
    - makes decisions independently, with little or no input from the rest of the group
    - privileges obedience, loyalty and strict adherence to rules
    - cultivates reliable and devoted followers
    - acts as the principal authority figure when it comes to establishing and maintaining order

The decision-making process is less creative under autocratic leadership, and leaders who abuse this style may be viewed as controlling, coercive, bossy, punitive, close-minded or dictatorial. This type of leadership is best applied in situations where there is little time for group decision-making.

2. Democratic leadership

   According to Lewin, democratic leadership is generally the most effective leadership style. A democratic leader

   - offers guidance to group members
   - acts as part of the group
   - encourages group members to participate but retains final say over the decision-making process

   Group members feel engaged in the process and are consequently more motivated and creative.

3. Laissez-faire leadership

   Lewin's researchers discovered that this type of leadership is generally the least effective style, because the laissez-faire leader

   - offers little or no guidance to group members
   - leaves the decision-making process up to group members
   - creates very poorly defined roles

   Under laissez-faire leaders, participants show little cooperation, lack motivation and make more demands on the leader.

Reflection

What impact will Lewin's work have on you and your team?

_____
_____
_____
_____
_____

Drucker's *The Effective Executive*

Drucker (2006) believes that employees are assets, not liabilities. He argues that knowledgeable workers are the essential ingredient of the modern economy, and a manager's job is to both prepare people to perform and give them freedom to so.

Each chapter of *The Effective Executive* focuses on one of seven tips and strategies that leaders need to know in order to achieve top performance and great results:

1. Effectiveness can be learned
2. Know thy time
3. What can I contribute?
4. Making strength productive
5. First things first
6. The elements of decision-making
7. Effective decisions

Fundamentally, effective executives

- work systematically at managing the limited time that they have
- focus on results, not effort
- build on strengths rather than weaknesses
- look for opportunities, not problems
- prioritise areas where superior performance will produce the best outcomes
- make decisions selectively and effectively

Reflection

What impact will Drucker's work have on you and on your team?

_____
_____
_____
_____
_____

Covey's seven habits of highly effective people

In his seminal book *The 7 Habits of Highly Effective People*, Covey (2013) lays out the seven things that successful people do to distinguish themselves from their less-successful peers. His argument is that by educating one's own conscience in an attempt to assume these fundamental habits of thought, anyone can become a highly effective person who routinely achieves their personal and professional goals.

The seven key cognitive habits identified by Covey in *The 7 Habits of Highly Effective People* are as follows:

1. Be proactive

    Proactive people focus their time, energy and attention on the things that they can control. They take responsibility for their own lives rather than blaming their problems on their genetics, upbringing or circumstances.

2. Begin with the end in mind

   This habit is based on the principle that all things are created twice; the mental creation is followed by the physical creation. Covey argues that by keeping the desired end result in mind, effective people are more likely to achieve their aims.

3. Put first things first

   Putting first things first is about life management as well as your purpose, values, roles and priorities. In this context, 'first things' are those that you personally find most worthwhile.

4. Think win/win

   People who think win/win see life as a cooperative arena, not a competitive one. A person who approaches conflicts with a win-win attitude possesses three vital character traits: integrity, maturity and abundance mentality.

5. Seek first to understand, then to be understood

   Communication is the most important skill in life, yet most people listen with the intent to reply rather than to understand. By contrast, effective leaders ensure that they are listening to and respecting the opinions of those whom they lead.

6. Synergise

   Synergy is the habit of creative cooperation. It is the process through which individuals combine their skills and experiences to produce better results than they could achieve on their own.

7. Sharpen the saw

   Sharpening the saw means taking care of 'the greatest asset you have – you' (Covey 2013). It involves striving for continuous improvement in the following areas:
   - physical – healthy eating, exercising and resting
   - social and emotional – making social and meaningful connections with others
   - mental – learning, reading, writing and teaching
   - spiritual – expanding the self through meditation or creative pursuits

Reflection

What impact will Covey's work have on you and your team?

_____
_____
_____
_____
_____

Fullan's six secrets of change

In *The Six Secrets of Change*, Fullan (2008) offers a blueprint that school leaders can use to guide action towards effective and long lasting changes. These changes will ultimately improve the culture of the organisation and its efficiency.

1. Love your employees

    Fullan argues that all the stakeholders in an organisation should be acknowledged as equally important. By recognising that employees are a leader's greatest asset, leaders can make sure to get the most out of their staff.

2. Connect peers with purpose

    A leader should act as a facilitator by connecting peers through meaningful working relationships. By promoting positive, purposeful peer interactions, leaders can cultivate collaboration between peers and encourage the flow of knowledge.

3. Capacity building prevails

    Building capacity in people enables leaders to become facilitators. Fullan stresses that when people are involved in continuous learning, leaders can worry less about management.

4. Learning is the work

    A commitment to ongoing professional learning is vital when it comes to building the capacity of an organisation. Therefore, Fullan believes that learning related to the work of the institution should be embedded in the context of the work itself. In this regard, professional development such as workshops and courses should be seen as an input to continuous learning and precision in teaching.

5. Transparency rules

    Transparency here refers to the continuous analysis of results. Fullan believes leaders should support schools to

    a. compare themselves with themselves (that is, compare the progress they are making now compared to previous years)
    b. compare themselves with their statistical counterparts
    c. examine their results relative to an external or absolute standard

    But he does not condone the use of league tables that display a comparison of the results of every school without regard for context.

6. Systems learn

    Fullan's first five secrets lay the foundation for a successful organisation: an organisation that learns from itself. This will happen when

    a. there are many leaders throughout the school who collaborate in order to provide continuity of learning and development

b. employees are valued – they are at the centre of the organisation, and they are connected to their peers through a common purpose with frequent opportunities to examine their practices and results
   c. the organisation is willing to constantly reflect on its practices and change its culture in order to improve system performance

Reflection

What impact will Fullan's work have on you and your team?

_____
_____
_____
_____
_____

Shackleton's Way by Morrell and Capparell

According to Morrell and Capparell's (2003) comparison of these early Antarctic explorers, Robert Falcon Scott and Ernest Shackleton demonstrated two very different leadership styles. Whereas Scott was dour, bullying and controlling, Shackleton was warm, humorous and egalitarian. Scott tried to orchestrate every movement of his men, while Shackleton gave his men responsibility and some measure of independence. Scott was secretive and untrusting; Shackleton talked openly and frankly with his men about all aspects of the work. Scott put his team at risk to achieve his goals, but Shackleton valued his team's lives above all else.

The following table sums up the contrasting character traits of the two men:

Scott	Shackleton
• ambitious • technically naive • hierarchical • arrogant • wary of colleagues more able than himself • indifferent selector • poor trainer • bad safety record • gifted writer	• single-minded • excellent in crisis • technically sensible • gregarious • excellent public speaker • good conceptual planner • effective selector and trainer • good safety record • bored by administration • politically astute

Table 1   Adapted with permission from Morrell and Capparell (2003)

Step 1: Find your philosophy of leadership

Whereas Scott's men all died on the way back from the South Pole, all of Shackleton's party survived the wreck of their ship, *Endurance*, in the crushing Antarctic ice. Even though they were stranded 12 000 miles from civilisation with no means of communication for almost two years, Shackleton and a few of his men endured an 800-mile trip across the frigid south Atlantic with little more than a rowboat to get help for his men, and all 27 of his crew made it out of Antarctica alive.

Here are some things we can learn from Shackleton's leadership:

- Cultivate a sense of compassion and responsibility for others.
- Once you commit, stick through the tough learning period.
- Do your part to help create an upbeat environment at work, as this is important for productivity.
- Broaden your cultural and social horizons by learning to see things from different perspectives.
- In a rapidly changing world, be willing to venture in new directions to seize opportunities and gain new skills.
- Find a way to turn setbacks and failures to your own advantage.
- Be bold in vision and careful in planning.
- Learn from past mistakes.
- Never insist on reaching a goal at any cost. The goal must be achieved without undue hardship for your staff.

Reflection

What have you learned from reading this comparison of Scott and Shackleton's leadership styles that will be useful to you and your team?

_____
_____
_____
_____
_____

Step 2
Create a Time Allocation Inventory

Based on my own involvement in designing, managing and evaluating a mentoring program at a large metropolitan primary school, I have firsthand knowledge that the implementation of such a program can be much more time-consuming than anticipated. This raises the critical issue of where observers are going to find the time to observe and provide feedback to teachers. Given that many schools will not have the funds to hire mentors or coaches, it is imperative that the observer works systematically at managing their time. After all, as Drucker famously said, 'Until we can manage time, we can manage nothing else'.

To assist observers with time management, Step 2 of the Pirozzo Process introduces an invaluable tool: the Time Allocation Inventory (pp. 15–17; available for download at **go.hbe.com.au**).

How to use the Time Allocation Inventory survey

Completing the Time Allocation Inventory survey (p. 15) is an extremely useful way for observers to get a handle on how well they manage their time. The inventory is designed to help you work out the percentage of time in a week that you devote to activities in each of the following five categories:

- maintenance
- professional
- community
- personal
- visualising and creating

Once you have answered the survey questions and calculated percentages, use the following key to decode your results:

- The amount of time dedicated to activity 1 indicates the percentage of time that you devote to *maintenance*.
- The amount of time dedicated to activities 2, 3, 4 and 5 indicates the percentage of time that you devote to *professional*.
- The amount of time dedicated to activity 6 indicates the percentage of time that you devote to *community*.
- The amount of time dedicated to activities 7, 8, 9, 10 and 11 indicates the percentage of time that you devote to *personal*.
- The amount of time dedicated to activities 12 and 13 indicates the percentage of time that you devote to *visualising and creating*.

How to use the Time Allocation Inventory pie charts

Now, transfer your results to the blank Time Allocation Inventory pie chart on page 16. Based on the results from your Time Allocation Inventory, colour in the pie chart provided below, indicating the percentage of time in a week (168 hours) that you devote to activities in each of the five categories.

Once you have coloured in your pie chart, you may like to compare your results with the ones to be found on the completed Time Allocation Inventory pie chart on page 17. These results derive from extensive research conducted with thousands of leaders and aspiring leaders in Australia, Canada, China, New Zealand, Singapore and the United Kingdom. They indicate the average amount of time that an observer should devote to activities in each of the five categories:

- maintenance – no more than 35 per cent
- professional – about 10 per cent
- community – about 5 per cent
- personal – about 30 per cent
- visualising and creating – at least 20 per cent

Obviously, percentages given reflects the average amount of time to be devoted to each of these categories, without taking into account individual circumstances such as parental leave or a death in the family.

Reflection

How similar or different are your results from the ones reported in the completed Time Allocation Inventory pie chart (p. 17)?

_____
_____
_____
_____
_____

Have another look at your results to see if any of the activities that you are presently involved in could be carried out by someone else within your team or year level. Leaders often believe that they need to be involved in everything that happens at the school, when in fact they could easily delegate some of their duties to others who would in turn benefit from the opportunity to show their leadership potential. The ability to delegate will be critical in your early days of taking the role as the observer, particularly if the school has no funds with which to hire a dedicated instructional coach.

Step 2: Create a Time Allocation Inventory

Time Allocation Inventory survey

In your future role as the observer, please estimate the total amount of time that you will devote to the following activities in the course of one week (168 hours).

Activity	Hours
1. maintenance (e.g. meetings, playground duties or emails)	
2. professional advancement (e.g. completing a qualification)	
3. professional memberships (e.g. Australian College of Educators)	
4. professional leadership (e.g. guest-speaking)	
5. coaching and mentoring (e.g. providing or receiving professional support)	
6. community commitments (e.g. Rotary Club)	
7. personal commitments (e.g. spending time with family)	
8. bodily requirements (e.g. sleeping and eating)	
9. sports (e.g. rugby or netball)	
10. hobbies (e.g. watching television or gardening)	
11. relaxation (e.g. meditating or massages)	
12. visualisation (e.g. new unit of study or unitised curriculum)	
13. creation (e.g. new interactive whiteboard activities)	
	Per cent (%)
How much of your time is devoted to activity 1?	
How much of your time is devoted to activities 2, 3, 4 and 5?	
How much of your time is devoted to activities 6?	
How much of your time is devoted to activities 7, 8, 9, 10 and 11?	
How much of your time is devoted to activities 12 and 13?	

Table 2

Implementing an Effective Teacher Feedback Program

Time Allocation Inventory pie chart

Based on the results of your Time Allocation Inventory survey (p. 15), colour in this pie chart to indicate the percentage of time in a week that you devote to

- maintenance
- professional
- community
- personal
- visualising and creating

Figure 2

Step 2: Create a Time Allocation Inventory

Time Allocation Inventory pie chart (completed)

Based on research conducted with thousands of leaders and aspiring leaders across Australia and New Zealand, I believe that this is the average amount of time in a week that a leader should spend on each activity:

- maintenance – no more than 35 per cent
- professional – about 10 per cent
- community – about 5 per cent
- personal – about 30 per cent
- visualising and creating – at least 20 per cent

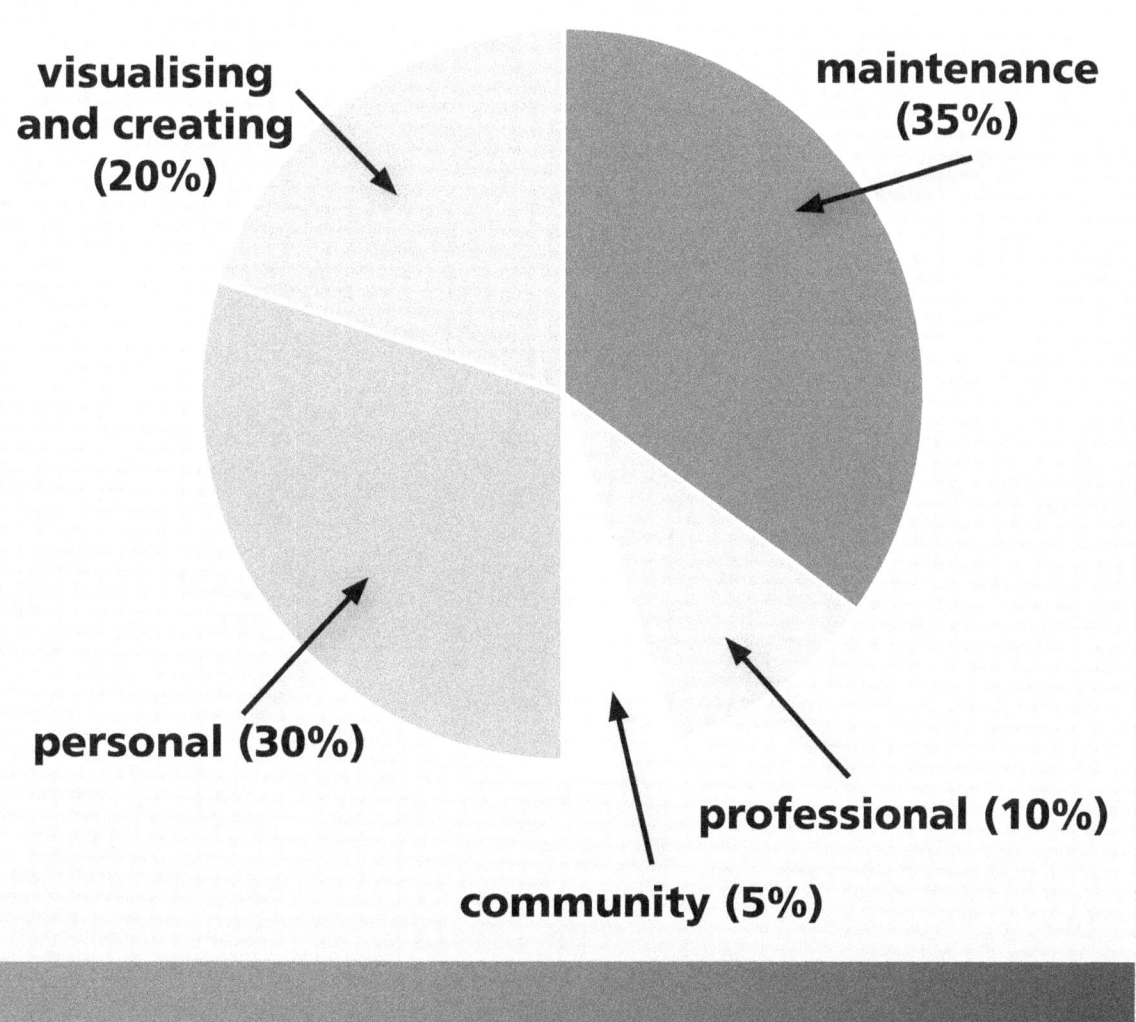

Figure 3

Step 3
Build knowledge of unit planning

In addition to establishing a clear leadership style and developing essential time-management skills, the observer should build an in-depth knowledge of unit planning. Based on my extensive work with more than 20 000 teachers in Australia, Canada, China, New Zealand, Singapore and the United Kingdom, this is an area in which many teachers seem to require assistance. Luckily, this is exactly what the Pirozzo Matrix was designed to do!

The Pirozzo Matrix

The story of the Pirozzo Matrix begins in 1985, when I first began working with Bloom's taxonomy and Gardner's multiple intelligences (Bloom 1984; Gardner 2011). Gradually, I came to realise that both theories had their own strengths and weaknesses:

- Bloom's taxonomy enables teachers to build depth and rigour in their teaching. It's great for nurturing students' thinking skills, but it does not fully provide for students' different learning styles.
- Gardner's theory of multiple intelligences enables teachers to cater to students' preferred learning styles. But it does not directly assist them to build depth and rigour in their units, lessons and classroom activities.

In relation to Bloom's taxonomy, it became clear to me that teachers needed access to a practical visual representation of this theory in order to identify quickly whether or not their students are employing lower-order thinking skills (LOTS) and higher-order thinking skills (HOTS). This is the reason why the Learning and Teaching Wheel (p. 20) was designed. The wheel shows how Bloom's six levels of thinking – plus a seventh level of my own devising – can be extrapolated using 92 critical verbs and 91 choices of project type.

To use the Learning and Teaching Wheel, start by selecting one of Bloom's seven levels, and then choose associated critical verbs. Match these verbs with some of the suggested project types to create classroom, homework and assessment activities that address one or more of the levels of Bloom's taxonomy; for example, an activity that operates at the level of Creating might require students to devise an experiment or compose a poem about an aspect of the unit topic. Typically, teachers will introduce a subject using activities at the LOTS levels of Knowing, Understanding and Applying, and then move on to HOTS – Analysing, Creating and Evaluating – once the LOTS have been mastered.

Once I was satisfied that we could easily build depth and rigour in our teaching, then we went searching for a model that would assist teachers in engaging their students. A very powerful theory that enables teachers to engage students through their preferred learning

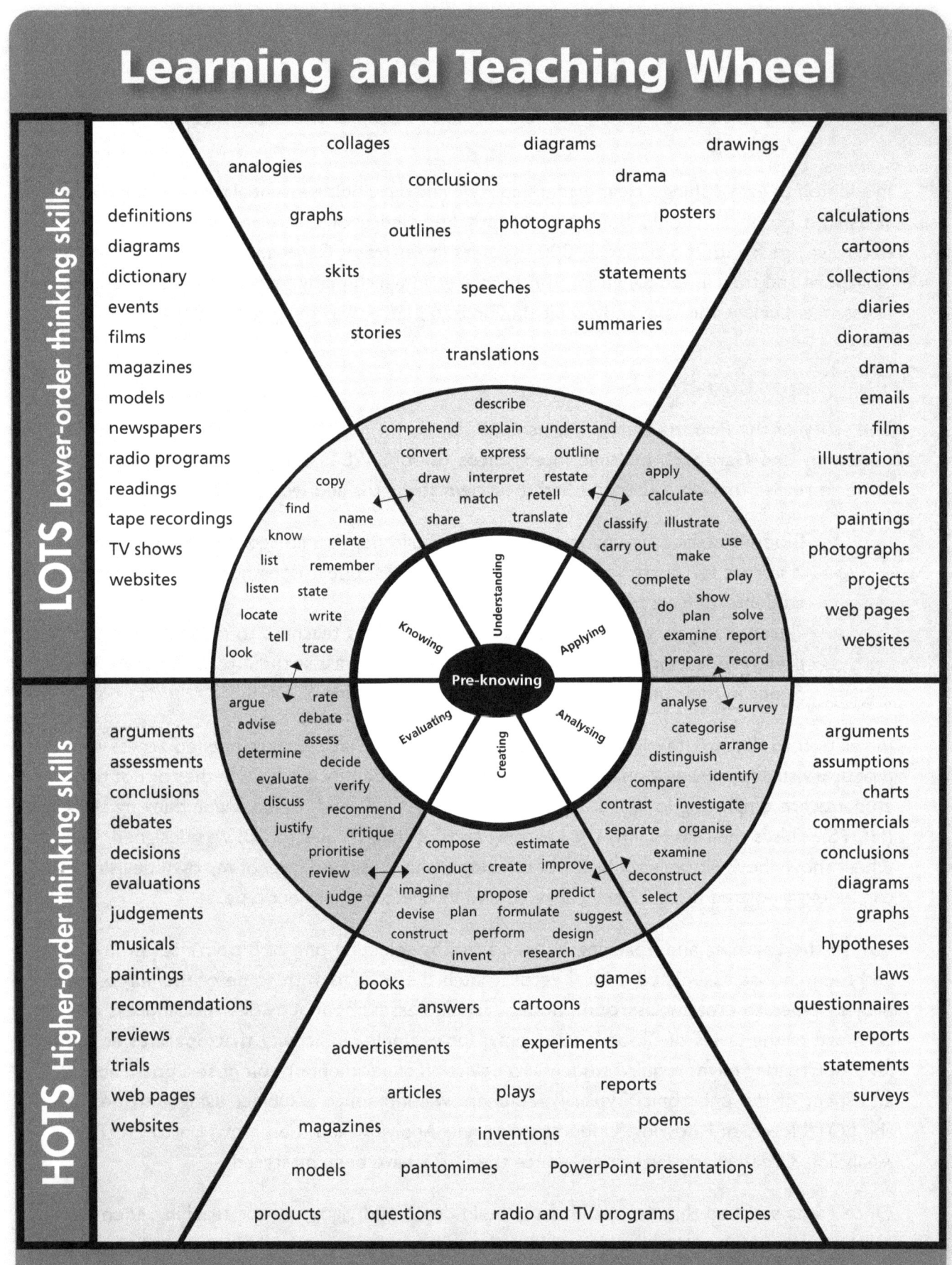

Figure 4   Adapted from Pirozzo (2007)

Step 3: Build knowledge of unit planning

styles is Gardner's multiple intelligence theory. In order to assist teachers to use the multiple intelligences theory, I developed the Engaging Wheel. This graphic representation of the multiple intelligences can be hung on the wall of the classroom to remind teachers of the characteristics of each intelligence.

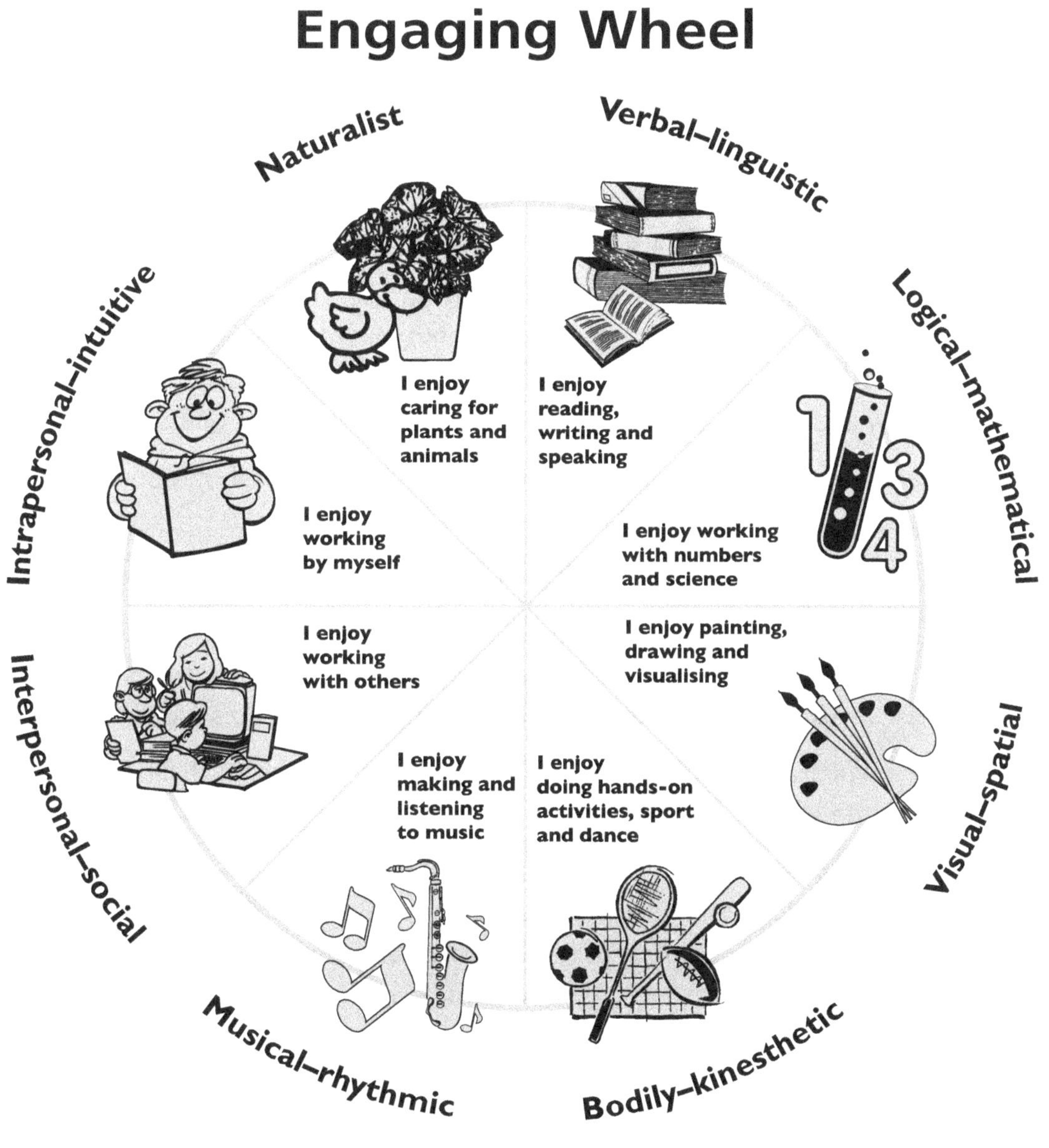

Engaging Wheel

Naturalist — I enjoy caring for plants and animals

Verbal–linguistic — I enjoy reading, writing and speaking

Logical–mathematical — I enjoy working with numbers and science

Visual–spatial — I enjoy painting, drawing and visualising

Bodily–kinesthetic — I enjoy doing hands-on activities, sport and dance

Musical–rhythmic — I enjoy making and listening to music

Interpersonal–social — I enjoy working with others

Intrapersonal–intuitive — I enjoy working by myself

Figure 5   Adapted from Pirozzo (2007)

Finally, I had an epiphany: Bloom's taxonomy and Gardner's multiple intelligences theory should in fact be integrated in order to take advantage of their strengths while eliminating their limitations. Why not have the best of both worlds by designing a strong planning framework that would enable teachers to have depth, rigour and engagement in their units and lessons? This is how the original 42-grid matrix was born. After Gardner's (1999) addition of an eighth intelligence, it was updated to the 48-grid matrix (p. 23). In 2004, following my decision to add a new sub-level, Pre-knowing, to Bloom's taxonomy, the matrix was updated to a 56-grid (p. 23).

How to use the Pirozzo Matrix

What is the process used by teachers to create a unit of work using the matrix? In order to achieve depth, rigour and engagement in our classroom, we encourage teachers to follow a 10-point planning process:

1. Identify the content descriptions from the Australian Curriculum on which you will base your unit.

2. Create RATs (Real Assessment Tasks) that the students need to complete in order to demonstrate the relevant content descriptions. These are the activities that the teacher will use for assessment and reporting purposes, and they should be located in the HOTS area (Pirozzo 2007). Colour the RATs yellow.

3. Develop a rubric for each RAT that can be used for teaching and assessment purposes. This 'backwards by design' approach (McTighe & Wiggins 2005) will ensure that students understand from the very beginning exactly what they have to know and be able to do to achieve mastery of the topic or concept.

4. Select critical verbs and related project types for each level of Bloom's taxonomy using the Learning and Teaching Wheel (p. 20).

5. Determine your students' preferred multiple intelligences using the Engaging Wheel (p. 21).

6. Use the matrix to create a number of cooperative learning activities based on the critical verbs selected in Step 4 and the multiple intelligences identified in Step 5.

7. Decide which aspects of the unit you will teach explicitly through direct instruction. Colour the explicit teachings blue.

8. Decide which activities are choices that you will offer to your students (for more information about teaching using choices, see Glasser 1986). Students can select which of these activities they'd like to complete, either by themselves or in groups, and so the choices provide the basis for differentiation. Leave the choices white.

9. Include a minimum of five different thinking tools (see pp. 27–34) that will help students to engage with the unit.

10. Assign a number to each activity to show the sequence in which you will teach this unit. This order will help to make sure that students have mastered prerequisite knowledge and skills before new information is introduced (Bruner 1966).

Two sample matrices have been provided as a model for teachers (pp. 24–25). While these appear in greyscale in this book, both samples as well as the blank 48- and 56-grid matrices are available in full colour as downloadable resources at **go.hbe.com.au**.

This chapter has discussed the use of the Pirozzo Matrix by teachers. For more information about how the matrix can be applied to classroom observation, see Step 7: Apply four strategies for providing effective feedback (pp. 53–75).

Step 3: Build knowledge of unit planning

48-grid planning matrix

Subject: Year: Unit:

Multiple intelligences	Bloom's taxonomy					
	KNOWING	UNDERSTANDING	APPLYING	ANALYSING	CREATING	EVALUATING
VERBAL — I enjoy reading, writing and speaking.						
MATHEMATICAL — I enjoy working with numbers and science.						
VISUAL/SPATIAL — I enjoy painting, drawing and visualising.						
KINESTHETIC — I enjoy doing hands-on activities, sports and dance.						
MUSICAL — I enjoy making and listening to music.						
INTERPERSONAL — I enjoy working with others.						
INTRAPERSONAL — I enjoy working by myself.						
NATURALIST — I enjoy caring for plants and animals.						

Content descriptions or essential learnings:

Figure 6   Adapted from Pirozzo (2007)

56-grid planning matrix

Subject: Year: Unit:

Multiple intelligences	Bloom's taxonomy						
	PRE-KNOWING	KNOWING	UNDERSTANDING	APPLYING	ANALYSING	CREATING	EVALUATING
VERBAL — I enjoy reading, writing and speaking.							
MATHEMATICAL — I enjoy working with numbers and science.							
VISUAL/SPATIAL — I enjoy painting, drawing and visualising.							
KINESTHETIC — I enjoy doing hands-on activities, sports and dance.							
MUSICAL — I enjoy making and listening to music.							
INTERPERSONAL — I enjoy working with others.							
INTRAPERSONAL — I enjoy working by myself.							
NATURALIST — I enjoy caring for plants and animals.							

Content descriptions or essential learnings:

Figure 7   Adapted from Pirozzo (2007)

Implementing an Effective Teacher Feedback Program

48-grid planning matrix

Unit: Saving the koala   **Subject:** Geography   **Year:** 8

Bloom's taxonomy

Multiple intelligences	KNOWING	UNDERSTANDING	APPLYING	ANALYSING	CREATING	EVALUATING
VERBAL — I enjoy reading, writing and speaking.	2. Carry out a **Thinking Cloud** and then list all the endangered species.	7. Explain why the whale has not become extinct.	19. Use the **BROW** strategy to prepare a TV/newspaper/radio ad to protect the koala.	18. Why should we prevent other species from becoming extinct?	**Real Assessment Task** — How will you prevent the koala from becoming extinct? Your action plan will be presented to various groups including students, teachers, administrators, parents, local government officials and a number of environmental experts	
MATHEMATICAL — I enjoy working with numbers and science.	4. Visit www.savethekoala.com to find out how many koalas there are at present.	9. Use **TREC** to estimate the cost of preventing the koala's extinction. Include costs for land, materials and labour.	23. Use **TAP** to brainstorm all the things that you can do to prevent the koala from becoming extinct.	24. Now, categorise the things that you can actually do to prevent the koala's extinction.		
VISUAL/SPATIAL — I enjoy painting, drawing and visualising.	1. Look at posters and photographs of extinct animals that your teacher brought to class.	5. Visit www.savethekoala.com. Draw a map to show where most koalas live.	16. Make a timeline of when dinosaurs were alive. Why did they become extinct?	25. Create a **Venn Diagram** of koalas versus whales. What do they have in common?	41. Create your own web page about saving the koala. Present it to your group and receive their feedback. You may choose the **LDC** tool as an evaluation strategy.	
KINESTHETIC — I enjoy doing hands-on activities, sports and dance.	10. Participate in an excursion to the local koala sanctuary and/or visit your local park.	13. Make cut-outs of your favourite endangered species.	17. Role play your favourite endangered species using a **W Chart**. Why have you selected this one?	20. Organise a poster, chart or collage for your favourite endangered species.	34. Create and perform a play dealing with tree clearing.	36. Devise an environmental game that could be used to teach others. **WASPS**
MUSICAL — I enjoy making and listening to music.	11. Learn a song about saving an endangered species.	14. Choose a song about people caring for the environment and explain its meaning to your group.	42. Choose the music to be played while presenting your action plan.	21. Arrange the music to be played while presenting your action plan.	26. Compose a rap, jingle or song to save the koala. **LEAP**	37. Act and choreograph a dance about saving the koala's habitat.
INTERPERSONAL — I enjoy working with others.	29. What can your group do to stop a species from becoming extinct? **TAP**	6. When is an animal endangered? Discuss this with your group.	33. Interview the manager of your local zoo to discover how they keep koalas alive.	31. Use **The Rake** to design a model of the best environment for the koala that its habitat has plenty of space for climbing, feeding, breeding and sleeping.	32. Present your ideas for the best environment for the koala to live in to your class. **LDC**	
INTRAPERSONAL — I enjoy working by myself.	8. Should we keep animals in zoos? What is your opinion?	22. Visualise yourself as an endangered species. How do you feel? Now, complete a **Y Chart**.	15. Imagine a day in the life of a koala. Now, write a story and publish it in the school newspaper. **BROW**	27. Share with your group your concerns about tree clearing. How can this be stopped? Who can help?	38. You are standing in front of a koala while its habitat is being destroyed. Now complete an **X Chart**.	40. Assess whether the koala will be extinct by the year 2020 by using the **SOWC Analysis**.
NATURALIST — I enjoy caring for plants and animals.	3. What would your life be without plants and animals? **TPSS**	12. How do you feel when you see a koala that has been rescued from a car accident on TV?	28. How would you promote the idea of preserving an endangered species?	35. Analyse the things that you can do to become more environmentally friendly.	30. Review *Where the Forest Meets the Sea*. Imagine you are the child in the book. **Y Chart**	39. Determine the impact of tree removal on the survival of the koala.

Content descriptions or essential learnings: Australian Curriculum: Geography for Year 8
- The human causes and effects of landscape degradation (ACHGK051)
- The ways of protecting significant landscapes (ACHGK052)

Figure 8   Adapted from Pirozzo (2007)

Step 3: Build knowledge of unit planning

56-grid planning matrix

Unit: Why learn about plants? **Subject:** Science **Year:** F–2, EAL/D and children with learning difficulties

Bloom's taxonomy

Multiple intelligences	PRE-KNOWING	KNOWING	UNDERSTANDING	APPLYING	ANALYSING	CREATING	EVALUATING
VERBAL I enjoy reading, writing and speaking.	**Types of plants** • trees • bushes • grass • flowers • shrubs **Verbs** • be • chop • cover • cut • die • dig • eat • grow • have • plant • put • water **Prepositions** • in • on • under • above • beside • between **Thinking tools** Teacher introduces students to the following thinking tools from *The Thinking School* (2013): • LDC • TAP • Y Chart • X Chart • PSDR • TPS • LEAP • Venn diagram	Name the parts of a plant.	Explain how plants grow.	Read a book about trees.	Analyse the book about trees. What did you like the most about this book? Why?	**RAT 1** Read *The Enormous Turnip*, then create your own narrative.	Read your narrative in front of the class and receive their feedback using the **LDC**.
MATHEMATICAL I enjoy working with numbers and science.		List all the known plants.	How many species of plant are there?	Examine the things that plants need in order to survive.	Discover how your plant grows.	Keep a record of your plant growth.	Evaluate the growth of your plant every week.
VISUAL/SPATIAL I enjoy painting, drawing and visualising.		Bring your favourite plant to class.	Draw your own plant.	Label the parts of your plant.	Compare the plants in your country with the plants that are found in Australia.	Design a Venn Diagram using the information that you already have.	Are the plants found in your country different to the ones found in Australia?
KINESTHETIC I enjoy doing hands-on activities, sports and dance.		Participate in an excursion to the botanical gardens or local park. **Y Chart**	Describe the different kind of plants that you saw during the excursion.	Walk around the school grounds and look at the plants.	Contrast the plants at your school with those you saw during an excursion. **Venn diagram**	**RAT 2** Create a box where you will be able to grow a small plant.	Evaluate the process of making your own box. How could you improve it? **TAP**
MUSICAL I enjoy making and listening to music.		Listen to songs about plants, forests and the environment.	Explain the meaning of your chosen song to your group.	Sing this song in English (for EAL/D students).	Using various instruments, begin to compose your own song or dance.	Create your own song or dance. **LEAP**	Present this song or dance to your class. **LDC**
INTERPERSONAL I enjoy working with others.		What did you like most about the excursion to the local gardens?	Share your thoughts with a partner. **TPS**	In your group, discuss the things that plants need to grow.	What would have happened if your plant did not receive any light? **PSDR**	**RAT 3** Devise an experiment to show what happens when plants don't receive any light.	How could you have improved your experiment? Share your suggestion with the class.
INTRAPERSONAL I enjoy working by myself.		Read simple worksheets about plants.	Complete simple worksheets about plants.	Match the words to the pictures.	Using the **Y** or **X Chart**, share with your team how you feel when a tree is cut down?	Create a dictionary of plants (in English and in your own language).	Using a dictionary, teach another student what you have learned about plants.
NATURALIST I enjoy caring for plants and animals.		List the parts of a plant (branch, trunk, flower, fruit, leaf, petals, roots, seeds and stem).	Explain why plants need the following things: light, soil, sun and water.	Examine why these animals are linked with plants: ant, bee, spider, butterfly and grasshopper.	Categorise the animals that are associated with plants.	Plant your favourite vegetable in the school garden.	What could you do to improve growing your vegetables? Advise your group or class.

Content descriptions or essential learnings:

Australian Curriculum: Science for Years F–2
- Science involves exploring and observing the world using the senses (ACSHE013)
- Living things have a variety of external features (ACSSU017)
- Living things live in different places where their needs are met (ACSSU211)
- People use science in their daily lives, including when caring for their environment and living things (ACSHE022)

Figure 9   Adapted from Pirozzo (2007)

Step 4
Learn to use a variety of thinking tools

In order to stimulate students' curiosity and promote reflection, every unit should involve a minimum of five different thinking tools. These should be referenced in the Pirozzo Matrix so that students can use them to increase their engagement level. Thinking tools help your students by

- enabling them to become more engaged in their learning
- assisting them in processing data and information
- providing them with a framework to generate and organise their ideas
- enabling them to transfer their knowledge from lower-order thinking skills (LOTS) to higher-order thinking skills (HOTS) (Pirozzo 2013, p. 1)

Leaders who assume the role of observer should have an in-depth knowledge of at least 25 thinking tools, since this will enable them to offer suggestions and refinements to those they observe. To this end, the Thinking Toolkit (p. 28) offers a selection of just some of the possibilities from which educators may choose. But of the innumerable thinking tools available, which ones are the most effective in the classroom? And which thinking tools have been useful to me in my role as observer in numerous schools?

For a more in-depth discussion of thinking tools and skills, see my book *The Thinking School: Implementing Thinking Skills Across the School* (Pirozzo 2013).

Thinking tools for the teacher

Here is a brief overview of some thinking tools that observers may wish to introduce to teachers during the feedback process to assist them in improving their practice.

Cooperative learning

Cooperative learning can be a wonderful way for students to work together to complete a task. But without a clear plan it has the potential to become noisy and unproductive. One way to avoid this is to teach students that every time the class performs a cooperative activity, they will take on a specific role. The following are cooperative learning roles that we have found very useful:

Gatherer	This student collects and returns all the material and equipment needed for a certain activity.
Encourager	This student supports the group with positive comments: 'Yes, we can do it!' The Encourager helps the group to work as a team.

Thinking Toolkit

A&R: *Action and Reaction*

ARC: *Action, Reaction, Consequences*

BROW: *Brainstorm, Read, Organise, Write*

BROWSE: *Brainstorm, Read, Organise, Write, Share, Evaluate*

Concept Maps: *A convergent thinking tool organiser*

DMT: *Decision Making Tool*

GLOW: *Gather, List, Organise, Write*

ISACS: *Identify, Share, Argue, Compromise, Solve*

ITPE: *Identify, Think, Pair, Explain*

IW⁵: *Why, Why, Who, What, What*

LDC: *Like, Dislike, Challenges or Changes*

LEADER: *Listen, Explain, Argue, Debate, Elaborate, Reflect*

LEAP: *Listen, Explain, Argue, Perform*

LIMACE: *Locate, Identify, Make, Analyse, Create, Evaluate*

LITE: *Like, Improvements, Time line, Evaluation*

MAC: *My Area of Control*

MACE: *Magnify, Act, Classify, Empathise*

PSDR: *Predict, Share, Do, Reflect*

RedMast: *Read, Estimate, Draw, Make, Arrange, Simplify, Think*

RIB-TT: *Ralph's Inquiry-Based Thinking Tool*

SCRAM: *Substitute, Create, Rewrite, Audition, Modify*

SCREAM: *Separate, Classify, Rate, Explain, Act, Magnify*

SOWC Analysis: *Strengths, Opportunities, Weakness & Consequences*

STIESA: *Show, Think, Imitate, Explore, Sound, Apply*

TAP: *Think All Possibilities*

TEAM: *Think, Explain, Arrange, Make*

The Rake: *Touch, Smell, Taste, Look, Listen, Think*

Thinking Clouds: *A divergent thinking tool organiser*

Trec: *Think, Read, Estimate, Calculate*

WASPS: *Watch, Ask, Show, Practise, Show*

WINCE: *Want, Identify, Need, Create, Evaluate*

W CHART: *Looks, Sounds, Feels, Tastes, Thinks*

X CHART: *Looks, Sounds, Feels, Thinks*

Y CHART: *Looks, Sounds, Feels,*

Figure 10   Adapted from Pirozzo (2013)

Step 4: Learn to use a variety of thinking tools

Timekeeper This student's job is to ensure that their group completes the activity on time. Once the teacher has informed the class that they have 10 minutes to complete their experiments, the Timekeeper works with their team to achieve this.

Reporter This student takes notes during the activity and then reports the findings of the experiment to the entire class.

It is advisable that students are assigned new roles on a rotating basis; otherwise, they will complain that they are constantly being asked to be the Reporter or Gatherer.

SCRAM

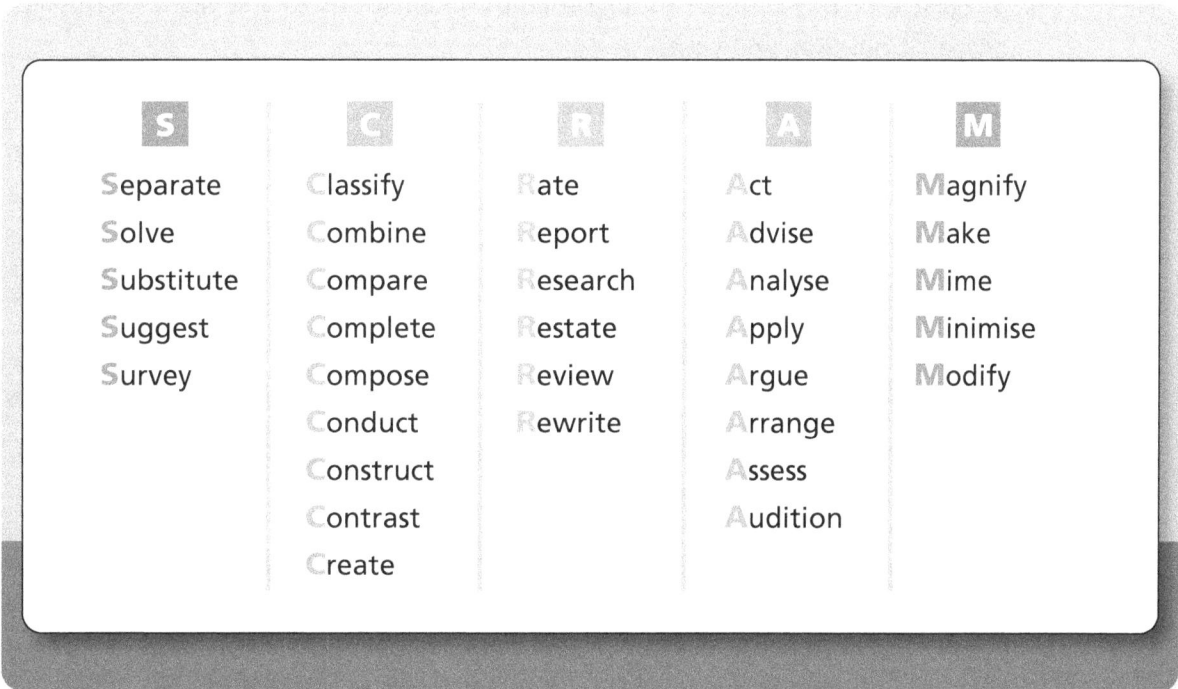

Figure 11   Adapted from Pirozzo (2007)

SCRAM was devised to assist teachers in promoting HOTS in their classrooms. It is a very versatile thinking tool because different verbs can be selected from each of the five columns depending on the activity in which students are involved.

Example 1: Harry Potter

In dealing with the character of Harry Potter, the teacher can set students the following tasks:

1. Substitute yourself in the role of Harry Potter.
2. a. Create a new cloak for Harry Potter
   b. Compose a rhyme for playing quidditch.
   c. Construct a poster for the Hogwarts Express.

3. a. Review the book.
    b. Research mythical creatures.
4. a. Audition for the role of Harry Potter
    b. Act out going through the trap door.
5. a. Mime movements while wearing the invisible cloak.
    b. Make a time line of events.

Example 2: Preparing risotto

In preparing risotto, the teacher is asking the students to do the following:

1. a. Survey the class on flavour preferences and combinations for rice dishes.
    b. Suggest a variety of different ingredient combinations to suit taste, availability, preparation, time and cost.
2. a. Create a risotto recipe that can be prepared using the microwave.
    b. Conduct an experiment to discover the most suitable rice for risotto making.
3. a. Research the types of rice available.
    b. Rate them according to their suitability for risotto making.
    c. Rewrite the recipe for younger students and add diagrams whenever possible.
4. a. Analyse the nutritional value of your risotto.
    b. Assess the suitability of your recipe for someone that is lactose intolerant.
5. a. Modify your recipe in order to reduce costs and energy consumption.
    b. Make your risotto dish and have your group or class evaluate it in terms of taste and presentation.

LEADER

LEADER was specifically designed to help teachers prepare their students for a debate by taking them through the six steps listed below:

1. Listen

   Team members listen to each other's ideas and brainstorm by using the thinking clouds. Each team member is given the opportunity to contribute to the discussion and argue their case.

2. Explain

   Team members explain what their ideas are and why they are worth considering.

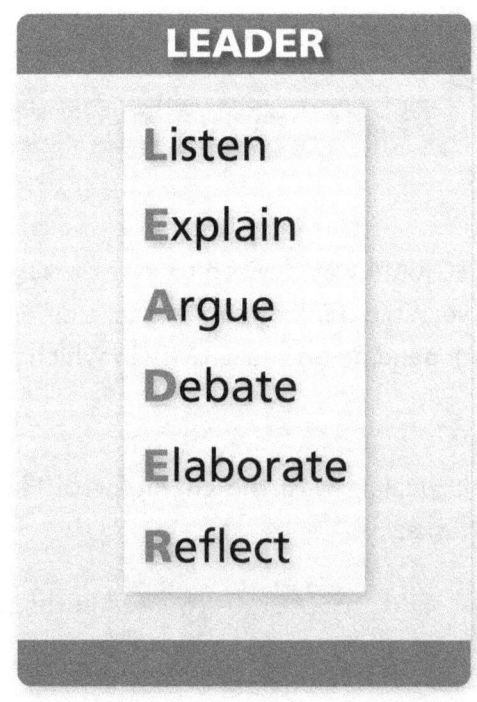

Figure 12   Adapted from Pirozzo (2013)

3. Argue

   The team works together to organise the arguments that they will put forward. They need to allocate each point to a speaker. Ideally the arguments should be split along a specific theme. For example:

   > The first speaker for the affirmative said that mobile phones should be banned in the classroom due to potential radiation poisoning. We in the negative believe this to be incorrect because there has not been a study that has conclusively shown that mobile phones usage increases risks of radiation poisoning.

4. Debate

   The team members debate their topic, taking into account possible rebuttal. The teacher should designate a set amount of time for each speaker, and the team members need to be aware of this when writing their debate.

5. Elaborate

   The team members elaborate on their arguments. Each individual begins to flesh out the ideas that they have been allocated. They need to gather factual evidence to support their ideas, not hearsay or personal opinions.

6. Reflect

   The team members reflect on what they have prepared both individually and as a team, and fine-tune any areas of concern.

PSDR

The PSDR method is most often employed to help students perform scientific experiments. It encourages students to go through a four-step thinking process:

1. Predict the outcome of an experiment.
2. Share their predictions with other students.
3. Do the experiment.
4. Reflect on the results of the experiment.

Example

1. Predict

   Predict what will happen when sodium hydroxide (NaOH) and hydrochloric acid (HCl) are mixed together in a beaker.

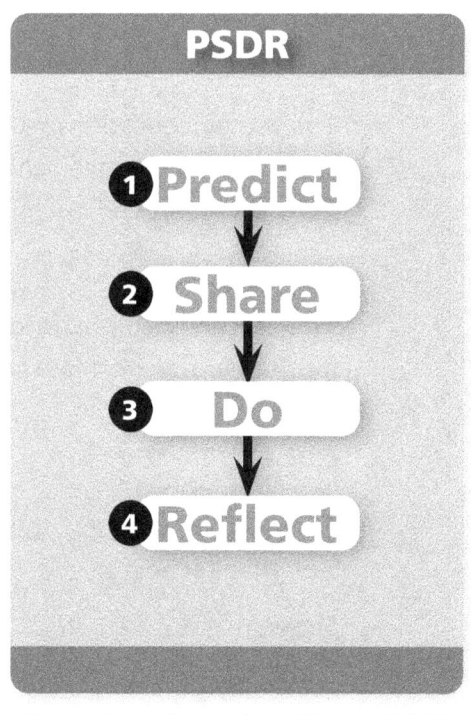

Figure 13   Adapted from Pirozzo (2007)

2. Share

    Share the factors that can impact on this experiment with your partner or group.

3. Do

    Do the experiment by adding 250 ml of NaOH and 300 ml of HCl. Be sure to follow all recommended safety procedures.

4. Reflect

    - Did you predict that a chemical reaction would take place and that sodium chloride (NaCl) and water (H2O) would be produced?
    - Is this a reversible chemical reaction?
    - If you were to increase the concentration of HCl, how would this affect the rate of the chemical reaction?

WASPS

WASPS works best with practical subjects like physical education and food technology. This example is for a physical education lesson on catching and throwing.

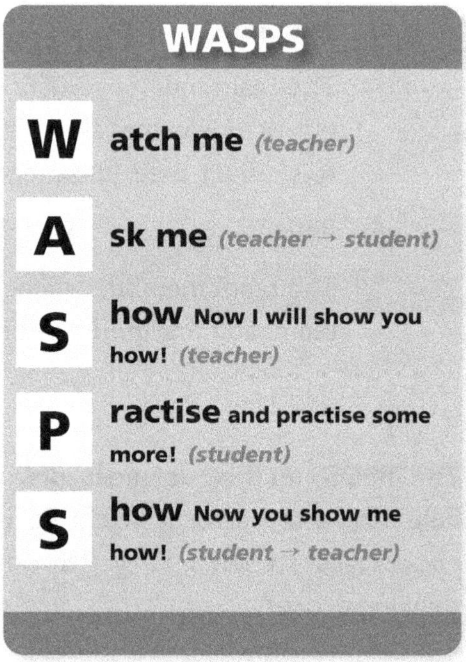

1. Watch me

    The teacher begins the lesson by explaining the technique that should be used to effectively catch the ball and throw it back to the receiver.

2. Ask me

    The teacher questions students: 'At what angle should my arm and shoulder be? Why should I bend my back?'

3. Show

    The teacher demonstrates the skill in slow motion and at normal speed. This operation should be repeated at least three times.

4. Practise

    The teacher provides the students with plenty of opportunity to practise their throwing technique.

5. Show

    Encourage the students to incorporate these skills into any game that uses this concept, such as T-ball or dodgeball. Modify the game to begin with so that students experience success. Then, once the students have developed very good

WASPS

W — atch me *(teacher)*

A — sk me *(teacher → student)*

S — how Now I will show you how! *(teacher)*

P — ractise and practise some more! *(student)*

S — how Now you show me how! *(student → teacher)*

Figure 14   Adapted from Pirozzo (2013)

hand-eye coordination, make the game more difficult by decreasing the size of the ball or increasing the field size or both.

Thinking tools for the observer

The following tools are especially useful for observers to use in their capacity as providers of feedback.

ARC

The ARC (Action, Reaction, Consequences) thinking tool is helpful when giving feedback to teachers who are encountering behavioural issues in their classrooms. It also provides observers with a way to model for teachers the best methods to deal with these issues.

Example

Felicity, a Year 7 student, sits by herself in an isolated area of the playground during morning and lunch breaks. Julie, a Year 9 student, regularly teases her. Eventually, Julie's teasing escalates to spreading rumours about Felicity's sexuality through emails, texts and social media. This is noticed by a teacher, who brings the issue to her head of department.

Based on the school's behaviour policy, the head of department decides to use ARC to deal with the situation. The resulting course of action is presented in Table 3 below.

Action	Reaction	Consequences
Julie's teasing has escalated to spreading rumours about Felicity's sexuality through emails, texts and social media.	Felicity has further withdrawn from the rest of the students. She feels insecure, vulnerable and worthless, and she is convinced that no one likes her. On a number of occasions, she has been heard saying, 'Life is just not worth living'.	The head of department advises Julie that a letter will be sent home to advise her parents of the situation. She will be kept in for detention after school for the next five days and she is expected to write a letter apologising to Felicity.

Table 3   Adapted from Pirozzo (2007)

LDC

LDC (Like, Dislike, Challenges or Changes) is a reflective thinking tool that enables the observer to provide feedback in a safe and structured manner.

- L   represents the good things about an idea
- D   signifies the negative aspects
- C   refers to aspects that are challenging or that can be modified

Example

L I liked that you included more than five different thinking tools in the unit.
D I didn't like that your unit contained so many LOTS activities but did not often progress to more advanced HOTS activities.
C To improve your unit, use the Pirozzo Matrix (see p. 23) to devise HOTS activities that will enable students to develop higher-order knowledge, skills and understandings.

X Chart

The X Chart can be used by both the teacher and the observer. The teacher can use the X Chart to help their students to deconstruct a character. For example, in dealing with the story of Cinderella, the teacher could be asking the following questions:

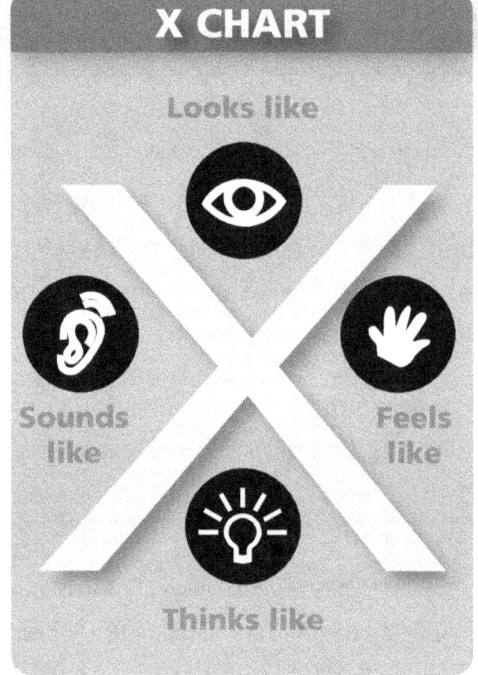

Figure 15 Adapted from Pirozzo (2007)

Looks like	Describe what Cinderella, the ugly sisters and the prince look like. You may like to draw them.
Feels like	Cinderella's stepmother tells her that she cannot attend the ball. If you were Cinderella, how would you feel? Explain.
Sounds like	Imagine that you were present when the prince finds out that the slipper fits Cinderella's foot. What would you hear? Write the dialogue between the prince and Cinderella.
Thinks like	The prince is asking Cinderella to marry him. Write a note, email or text describing what Cinderella is thinking at this moment.

The observer, on the other hand, can use the X Chart to come to grips with the leadership skills that they must develop in order to provide effective feedback.

Looks like	confident, interested, professional, reliable, facilitator
Feels like	affirmed, valued, empowered, confident, trusted, belonging, inspired
Sounds like	encouraging, stays on task, follows through, reasonable, caring, supportive, friendly
Thinks like	understood, appreciated, valued, integral part of the team

Step 5
Develop conflict-resolution skills

The observer may encounter difficulties depending on how the teacher accepts their feedback. For example, how will the observer react if the teacher receiving feedback

- is rude, aggressive and argumentative?
- refuses to have the observer in their classrooms?
- leaves the room while the observer is talking?
- agrees with the observer but makes no attempt to alter their teaching practice?

Step 5 is designed to help observers build the conflict-resolution skills necessary to deal with these and other challenges that arise during the observation and feedback process.

Why does conflict occur?

Conflict arises from differences between two people. It occurs whenever individuals disagree over their values, motivations, perceptions, ideas or desires. In relation to the observer-teacher relationship that is the focus of this book, conflict is defined as a disagreement in which the teacher perceives a threat to their professional integrity. Although conflict is a normal part of any professional relationship, it can escalate and become destructive if not handled quickly and appropriately.

In schools, we are not there to build houses or sell cars or manufacture golden chandeliers. We are there for one reason and one reason alone: to maximise the learning potential of every student. As this requires the input of many diverse individuals – including teachers, administrators, support staff and maintenance staff – the process of team-building is critical. The last thing schools want is to have the team dynamic disrupted by disagreements between observers and teachers. If unresolved, these disagreements will have a negative effect on how teachers relate to other staff members and perform their duties in the classroom, causing the children's education to suffer.

In the observer-teacher relationship, conflict often results from the teacher's perception that the feedback is unfair and doesn't reflect their true capabilities. In this scenario, feedback threatens the teacher's view of themselves and how they are perceived by others. This threat to the teacher's self-concept can be particularly devastating if the negative report is received while other unhappy events are taking place in the teacher's life, such as the loss of a loved one or a breakdown in their personal relationships.

Obviously, this kind of conflict cannot be left unchecked, as it will fester and eventually create a very unpleasant and unproductive working environment. For this reason, learning to manage conflict is a key skill for anyone who works in a team or has a supervisory role.

How can observers provide effective feedback while building professional relationships rather than harming them? How can they be sure to execute the strategy that is best suited to their specific conflict situation? From my extensive experience in coaching and mentoring educators, I have found that if the observer is going to solve conflicts successfully, then they need to know their own conflict resolution style as well as that of the teacher receiving the feedback.

Conflict resolution styles

In 1974, Kenneth Thomas and Ralph Kilmann (1974) developed the Thomas-Kilmann Conflict Mode Instrument (TKI). Basically, this model assumes that individuals deal with conflict based on two underlying dimensions: concern for self (assertiveness) and concern for others (cooperativeness).

The Thomas-Kilmann model illustrates the options we have when handling conflict. There are two dimensions in the model. The first dimension, assertiveness, is concerned with conflict responses based on our attempt to get what we want. The other dimension, cooperativeness, is concerned with responses based on helping others get what they want. By plotting assertiveness and cooperativeness on two axes, the TKI generates five options for dealing with conflict:

- avoiding
- accommodating
- competing
- compromising
- collaborating

Avoiding conflict style (no winners/no losers)

Avoiding is both unassertive and uncooperative. Individuals who use this mode tend to sidestep the conflict without trying to satisfy either person's concerns (Thomas & Kilmann 1974).

The avoiding style is characterised by inaction. It is typically used when a teacher has reduced concern for their own welfare as well as for the welfare of others. Some behaviours associated with this conflict style are withdrawal, stonewalling, shutting down and being unwilling to expose oneself to ridicule.

During conflict, avoidant teachers adopt a 'wait and see' attitude, often hoping that the conflict will disappear on its own without their involvement (Bayazit & Mannix 2003). Unfortunately, by leaving the conflict unresolved, the individual may allow the problem to get out of control. Obviously, this is an ineffective approach to take when it comes to solving high-stakes conflicts.

According to Culbertson (2014) this conflict style should be used when

- the conflict is small and relationships are at stake
- you're counting to 10 to cool off
- more important issues are pressing and you feel you don't have time to deal with this particular one
- you have no power and you see no chance of getting your concerns met
- you are too emotionally involved and others around you can solve the conflict more successfully
- more information is needed

The drawbacks of this conflict style are as follows:

- Important decisions may be made by default.
- Postponing may make matters worse.

Accommodating conflict style (I lose/you win)

Accommodating is unassertive and cooperative. Individuals who use this mode attempt to satisfy the other person's concerns at the expense of their own (Thomas & Kilmann 1974).

The accommodating conflict style is characterised by high concern for others but low concern for oneself. Teachers who adopt this passive approach tend to derive personal satisfaction from meeting the needs of others and maintaining stable, positive social relationships (Forsyth 2013).

When faced with conflict, teachers with an accommodating conflict style tend to give in to the observer's demands out of respect for the social relationship. In schools, this could easily happen when a shy first-year teacher is being observed by a forceful, experienced and well-regarded teacher or a member of the leadership team.

Individuals who too frequently employ the accommodating style can appear weak and indecisive, without firm values or convictions. As a general rule, this approach is unlikely to generate the best outcome for both participants in the conflict.

According to Culbertson (2014) this conflict style should be used when

- an issue is not as important to you as it is to the other person
- you realise you are wrong
- you are willing to let others learn by making mistakes
- you know you cannot win
- it is not the right time and you would prefer to simply build credit for the future
- harmony is extremely important
- what the parties have in common is a good deal more important than their differences

The drawbacks of this conflict style are as follows:

- One's own ideas don't get attention.
- Credibility and influence can be lost.

Competing conflict style (I win/you lose)

Competing is assertive and uncooperative. Individuals who use this mode try to satisfy their own concerns at the other's person expense (Thomas & Kilmann 1974). In other words, they do anything to win!

Individuals who resort to this conflict style enjoy dominating others and typically see conflict as a 'win or lose' predicament (Forsyth 2013). These 'fighters' tend to force others to accept their personal views by employing competitive power tactics; they may argue, insult, accuse, undermine or even use violence.

Fortunately, teachers are unlikely to act violently while at school, but intimidating tactics can still be an issue. The competing style is especially likely to manifest if the teacher is an older member of the staff and is being observed by a much younger yet more academically qualified teacher or school leader.

The competing style can leave individuals feeling resentful, and misuse of the style can disempower others. Competing may offer short-term rewards, but it causes long-term detrimental effects.

According to Culbertson (2014) this conflict style should be used when

- you know you are right
- time is short and a quick decision is needed
- a strong personality is trying to steamroll you and you don't want to be taken advantage of
- you need to stand up for your rights

The drawbacks of this conflict style are as follows:

- This style can escalate conflict.
- Losers may retaliate.

Compromising conflict style (I win some/you lose some)

Compromising is intermediate in both assertiveness and cooperativeness. Individuals who use this mode try to find an acceptable settlement that partially satisfies both persons' concerns (Thomas & Kilmann 1974). This involves give-and-take from both individuals in order to reach a quick solution that doesn't fully satisfy either party.

Compromising teachers value fairness and prefer mutual give-and-take interactions. They believe that if they accept some of their opponent's demands, their agreeableness will encourage the other party to meet them halfway, in this way resolving the conflict (Van de Vliert & Euwema 1994).

According to Culbertson (2014) this conflict style should be used when

- people of equal status are equally committed to goals
- time can be saved by reaching intermediate settlements on individual parts of complex issues
- goals are moderately important

The drawbacks of this conflict style are as follows:

- Important values and long-term objectives can be derailed in the process.
- The style may not work if initial demands are too great.
- The style can spawn cynicism, especially if there's no commitment to honour the compromise solutions.

Collaborating conflict style (I win/you win)

Collaborating is both assertive and cooperative. Individuals who use this mode try to find a win-win solution that completely satisfies the concerns of both parties (Thomas & Kilmann 1974).

This conflict style is characterised by concern for oneself and others. During conflict, collaborating individuals work with the opposing party and others to find an amicable solution (Goldfien & Robbennolt 2007). By seeing conflict as a creative opportunity, these teachers willingly invest time and resources to ensure a 'win-win' outcome.

Teachers with this type of conflict style tend to be highly assertive and highly empathetic at the same time. In addition, successful employment of the collaborating style also requires developed conflict-resolution skills, mutual respect, a willingness to listen to others and the ability to discover many different solutions.

According to Culbertson (2014) this conflict style should be used when

- there is a high level of trust
- you don't want to have full responsibility
- you want others to also have 'ownership' of solutions
- the people involved are willing to change their thinking as more information is found and new options are suggested
- you need to work through animosity and hard feelings

The drawbacks of this conflict style are as follows:

- The process takes lots of time and energy.
- Some may take advantage of other people's trust and openness.

Culbertson (2014) concludes that none of these five conflict resolution styles is a 'one-size-fits-all' solution. In fact, which one is the best in a given situation will depend on a variety of factors, including the level of conflict. It follows that individuals can choose to adopt one or more of these conflict resolution skill depending on the context and the person with whom they are dealing.

A formal process to resolve conflict

Familiarity with the five different conflict resolution styles is very valuable to the observer, as they can select the most appropriate way to manage the teacher's behaviour.

Unfortunately, there will be times when the differences between the observer and the teacher are too great to bridge without formal intervention. This will require the observer and the teacher to have a face-to-face meeting and go through the following eight steps, drawn from the work of Hunt (2012) and Weeks (1992):

1. Call a formal meeting.
2. Establish discussion rules.
3. Identify the conflict.
4. Brainstorm a number of possible solutions.
5. Select a mutually beneficial solution.
6. Develop an action plan.
7. Implement the action plan.
8. Evaluate the conflict resolution process.

1. Call a formal meeting

Both the observer and the teacher must attend the meeting. If necessary, invite an unbiased third party such as a facilitator or mediator.

In order to have a constructive conversation, find a mutually-agreed safe place where the observer and the teacher feel that they can communicate honestly.

Ensure that the time scheduled for the meeting is acceptable to both parties while allowing enough time for meaningful discussion to take place. There is no point in trying to solve a difficult issue in 15 minutes! In many cases, a number of meetings may be required to solve the conflict.

2. Establish discussion rules

The observer and the teacher should agree upon a set of basic ground rules that will enable civil dialogue, such as the following:

- One person speaks at a time.
- A sincere commitment is made to listen to the other person before responding.

- Unless there is an explicit agreement to the contrary, the discussions are to be kept strictly confidential.
- Talk directly with the person with whom you have the conflict rather than seeking to involve others in gossip or alliance-building.
- Agree to try your hardest to solve the conflict.
- Agree to attack the issues and not the person with whom you disagree.
- Above all, ensure that the feelings of both parties are taken seriously.

3. Identify the conflict

The most important step in solving any conflict is to clearly define the conflict itself. It is important to make sure that both the observer and the teacher have the opportunity to define their needs in a way that is fully understood by the other person. Check for understanding before proceeding further with the process.

As Covey (2004) writes, it is best to 'seek first to understand, then to be understood'. In other words, it is critical to use active listening skills such as the following:

- Encourage the other person to share their feelings as honestly as possible.
- Clarify the issue rather than making assumptions.
- Restate what you have heard to make sure that you have understood what the other person has said.
- Stay focused on the ideas and feelings that really matter to you.
- Clearly state what you expect will happen as a result of this meeting.
- Be prepared for possible defensive responses to your assertions.
- Apply active listening skills.

4. Brainstorm a number of possible solutions

Brainstorm several possible solutions to the problem. Deal with one issue at a time, starting with the issue that both the observer and the teacher agree is most urgently in need of resolution.

Make sure that the observer and the teacher have a clear idea of what they expect to happen as the outcome of the meeting. This is important, as participants may have very different ideas about what constitutes a fair and reasonable solution. Summarise ideas in writing and restate them to each other to ensure that both parties agree with the solutions being discussed.

5. Select a mutually beneficial solution

Select the solution that best meets the needs of both the observer and the teacher. It is important that the solution is not imposed, but that the two participants arrive at it by themselves or with the guidance of a facilitator or mediator.

6. Develop an action plan

Once negotiations have concluded, it is important to register in writing the areas that have been agreed on. Ensure that the agreement is fair and balanced, meaning that it doesn't favour either the observer or the teacher. It should also be realistic enough that it will serve to prevent the conflict from flaring up again and again.

Based on this written agreement, the observer and the teacher are ready to formulate their action plan. In this plan they will need to clearly specify

- the goals that they would like to accomplish
- the dates by which these goals will be achieved
- the incremental steps that will lead to the achievement of the goals
- the monitoring and evaluation of this action plan

7. Implement the action plan

Implement the action plan by answering the following questions:

- Who will monitor the implementation of this action plan?
- Who will receive the updates that result from this monitoring process?
- What activities will be undertaken, and by whom?
- By what date will these activities be completed?
- Will the observer and the teacher meet on a regular basis to review how the action plan is progressing?
- Will there be any costs involved? Who will pay for these costs?

8. Evaluate the conflict-resolution process

Evaluate the conflict-resolution process by answering the following questions:

- Did the mediation process produce effective and lasting positive results for both the observer and the teacher?
- Were both participants satisfied with the resolution?
- Will the resolution eliminate or at least minimise the recurrence of conflict?

Reflection

When faced with conflict between the observer and a teacher, we are dealing with two professional individuals who share a common bond: They are both passionate about maximising the learning potential of every student in their classroom. What they may disagree on is how to get there! Each party will have their own beliefs regarding best practice in relation to everything from teaching reading to handling behavioural issues. There may even be differences of opinion regarding whether the children's desks should be arranged in straight rows or in clusters.

Ultimately, then, it shouldn't come as a surprise that there will at times be differences of opinion between observers and teachers. Teaching is a great profession because it fosters and values differing viewpoints, which is exactly what is needed for conflict to occur.

What is critical is that conflicts should not be allowed to fester, as this can create a very unpleasant and unproductive working environment. Conflicts should always be dealt with immediately and appropriately, preventing them for spreading throughout the school and damaging relationships that have taken a long time to build.

Step 6
Launch an effective teacher feedback program

If your feedback program is going to thrive, it must be implemented on a school-wide basis. It should be an integral part of a school's culture, and it should aim to involve the whole school community. If the program is not widely known or is accessible to only a few, it will generate suspicion, animosity and resistance that may ultimately lead to its demise.

In formulating a plan to establish an effective feedback program at your school, you should collect a good deal of data:

- Is there an effective feedback program already operating at your school?
- What are its goals?
- How long has it been operating?
- How successful is it?
- Who is responsible for its operation, monitoring and evaluation?
- How many teachers are involved?
- How well-resourced is it in terms of time allocation, personnel and funds?
- How well-supported is it from the administrative team?

After collecting this data, you can begin to analyse it with the goal of ensuring that its implementation is smooth and successful while remaining time- and cost-effective.

Rogers' diffusion of innovation theory

According to Clarke (1999), some inventions – like the Sony Walkman – take the world by storm. Others, like the fax machine, seem to fail and lie dormant for decades, but when their time comes, their use spreads rapidly. Similarly, some teacher feedback programs are slow to be adopted, others grow quickly in popularity, and still others never get past the planning stage. So, what are the factors that determine whether or not a new idea, model or program is going to be accepted by a school and the rate at which its acceptance will grow?

To understand the relationship between innovations and their implementation, we can turn to the theory popularised by Everett Rogers (2003) in his influential book *Diffusion of Innovations*. This framework describes the patterns of adoption and predicts whether and how a new idea will be successful. According to Rogers, 'an innovation is an idea, practice, or project that is perceived as new by an individual or other unit of adoption' (p. 12). The word 'perceived' emphasises the fact that an item may have been invented a long time ago, but if it is widely conceived of as new then it still counts as an innovation.

I believe that Rogers's diffusion of innovations theory is appropriate for investigating the implementation of a teacher effective feedback program in schools because it lists the five qualities that determine the success of an innovation:

1. Relative advantage

    Is this program perceived to be better than what we have at present? By being involved in it, will teachers receive any economic advantage, social prestige, convenience or professional satisfaction?

2. Compatibility

    Do the teachers perceive this program to be consistent with their values, past experiences and needs?

3. Simplicity

    Is this program easy to understand and to implement?

4. Trialability

    Are teachers able to trial this program on a limited basis?

5. Observability

    Once this program has been implemented, will teachers see immediate results?

In summary, potential adopters will evaluate an innovation based on its relative advantage compared to what they are doing at present.

Key to Rogers's diffusion of innovations theory is the notion that not all individuals will adopt a new behaviour, program or product simultaneously – a fact borne out by my own experience as an educational consultant and school leader. This means that teachers that adopt this new program early have different characteristics than those that will adopt it later. Developing an understanding of these characteristics can be crucial when predicting how your staff will take to the implementation of a new teacher feedback program.

Over many years of research, Rogers has identified the following five different personality traits that help us to reflect on how people will accept a new innovation:

1. Innovators
2. Early adopters
3. Early majority
4. Late majority
5. Laggards

1. Innovators

Innovators make up about 2.5 per cent of the population. They have the following characteristics:

Step 6: Launch an effective teacher feedback program

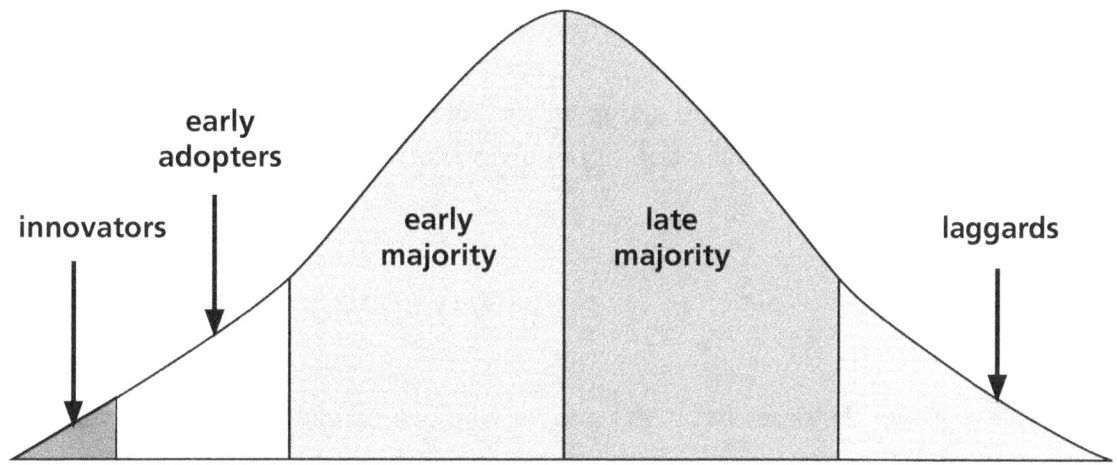

Figure 16   Adapted with permission from Rogers (2003, p. 281)

- They are the first and fastest group to adopt an innovation.
- They are willing to take risks and eager to try new ideas.
- They will adopt the program quickly, especially if it gives them kudos among other innovators.
- Because they are great communicators, they will play an important role in promoting the program among their colleagues.
- These are the teachers who, as soon as you propose this idea, will yell, 'This is awesome! I have been waiting to be involved in this type of program for a very long time! Let's waste no more time! Let's have a go!'

2. Early adopters

The early adopters make up about 13.5 per cent of the population. They have the following characteristics:

- Early adopters are the second fastest group when it comes to adopting an innovation.
- Because they are forward-thinking but less radical than innovators, early adopters are opinion leaders. Other members of the school will seek their advice regarding whether or not the program should be implemented.

- Early adopters are also essential to the adoption of the program because they will test it and provide feedback in order to improve it.
- They are an easy audience to persuade because they are constantly looking for new programs that will provide them social advantage. They like to be seen as trendsetters, so social prestige is one of their biggest drivers.
- For a new idea to be successful, it must attract both innovators and early adopters, as their acceptance will influence the early majority, late majority and laggards.
- Strategies to appeal to this group will include providing manuals and data about implementation and evaluation of the program.

3. Early majority

The early majority make up about 34 per cent of the population. They have the following characteristics:

- As a group, they are thoughtful people who are careful about accepting change and averse to taking risks.
- They will watch the early adopters carefully and deliberate for some time before adopting a new idea.
- They are neither the first nor the last to adopt an innovation. Their decision-making takes more time than the innovators and early adopters.
- They dislike complexity, so they will only implement this program if it is simple, delivers results quickly and requires minimum disruption to their teaching routine.
- They seek market leaders and have a strong sense of brand loyalty. Once they find that something works, they stick with it and do not change easily.
- Convincing the early majority will require ongoing evidence from credible individuals, as well as reports, newsletters and demonstrations. This group tends to rely on recommendations from others to guide their decision-making.

4. Late majority

The late majority make up about 34 per cent of the population. They have the following characteristics:

- The late majority are sceptical about change and will only adopt an innovation due to peer pressure. It takes them a long time to embrace a new innovation, and they do so with a great deal of resistance.
- In contrast to the innovators, who are risk takers, these teachers are cautious and risk-averse.
- Typically, the late majority adopt a new program because they feel that everyone else is doing it and they fear being left behind. They can be persuaded to adopt an innovation, but peer pressure is usually necessary.
- The late majority rely primarily on recommendations from colleagues, friends, neighbours and relatives.

- They are not swayed by advertising, but they are often influenced by the resistant opinions of the laggards.
- Strategies to appeal to this group include information on how many other teachers have tried the program and found it to be successful. It will also be important to emphasise the risk of being left behind.

5. Laggards

Laggards make up about 16 per cent of the population. They have the following characteristics:

- As a group, laggards are conservative, traditional and critical towards new ideas.
- They are the hardest group to bring on board because they are sceptical of change and see a high risk in adopting a new product or behaviour.
- Laggards are the last group to adopt an innovation. It is sometimes the case that by the time the laggards have finally decided to adopt a program, it has already been superseded or abandoned.
- Laggards tend to be influenced only by family, close friends and other laggards.
- Strategies to appeal to this group include giving them high levels of personal control over when, where and how they will embrace the new program. You might also show laggard staff members how other laggards have successfully adopted this idea, and use statistics, fear appeal and pressure from other groups.

Force field analysis

In addition to knowing the five different personality traits that help school leaders to reflect on how teachers will accept this new program, I believe that schools should also carry out a force field analysis (Lewin 1943). This is a method of listing, discussing and assessing the various forces for or against a proposed change. It is a team-building tool aimed at identifying and mitigating the forces that must be addressed if change is to be successful. Usually, the end goal of force field analysis is to overcome resistance to implementation.

Forces that help you to achieve the desired change are called 'driving forces' and those that work against the change are referred to as 'restraining forces'. Here are some types of forces to consider:

- administrative support
- teachers' attitudes
- present practices
- regulations
- traditions
- vested interests
- organisational structures
- available personnel
- time constraints
- costs and funding arrangements for implementation

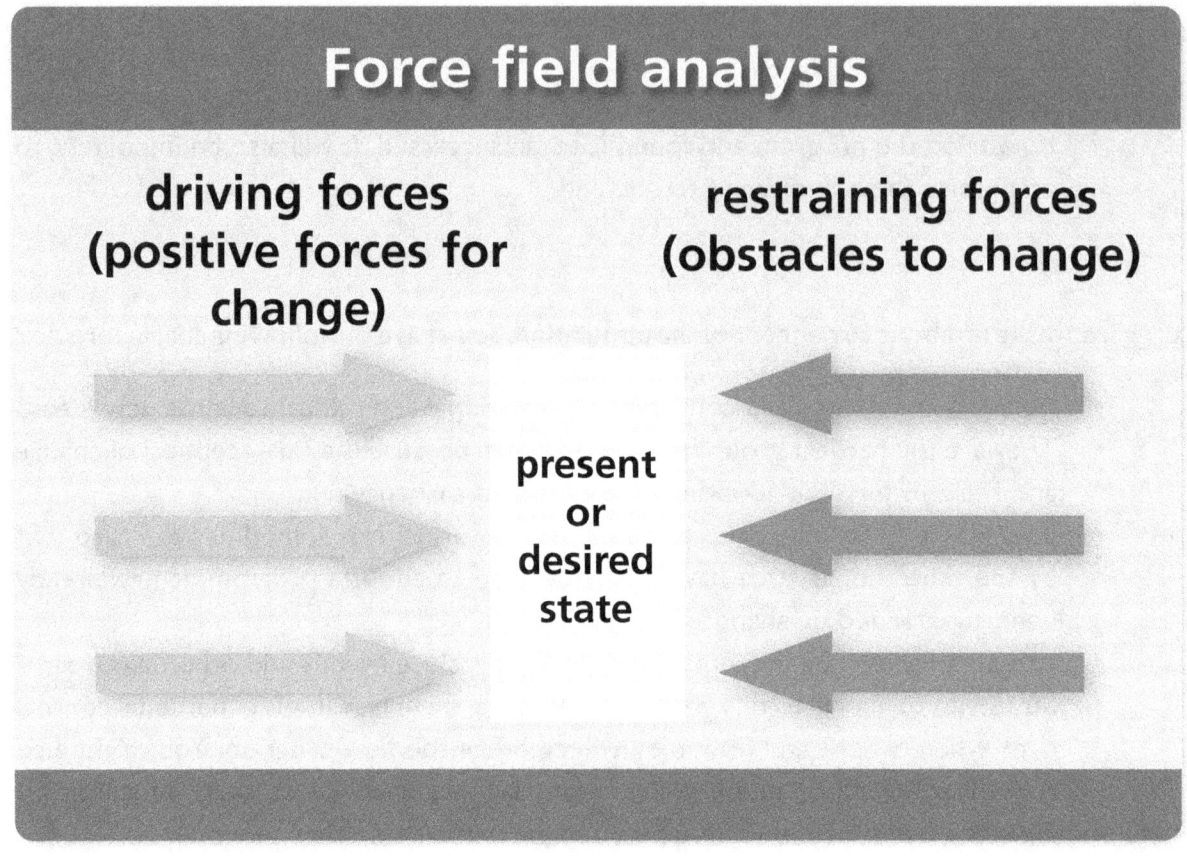

Figure 17   Adapted from Lewin (1943)

To complete a force field analysis, follow these steps:

1. Define the problem. What is the nature of your current situation that needs to be changed?

2. State clearly what you would like to achieve. In the force field analysis template opposite, the aim has been completed for you: 'Launch an effective teacher feedback program.'

3. Identify the driving forces and place them on the chart as labelled arrows. The length of the arrow reflects the relative strength of each force.

4. Identify the restraining forces and place them on the chart as labelled arrows. The length of the arrow reflects the relative strength of each force.

5. Predict some unintended consequences that might occur if the forces were altered, such as the formation of new alliances or increased levels of anxiety for some staff members.

6. Decide if the change is feasible. I would suggest that unless the driving forces add up to at least 65 per cent, the implementation of this feedback program will not be successful.

7. If you have decided that the change is feasible, then continue to strengthen the positive forces, weaken the negative ones and create new positive forces.

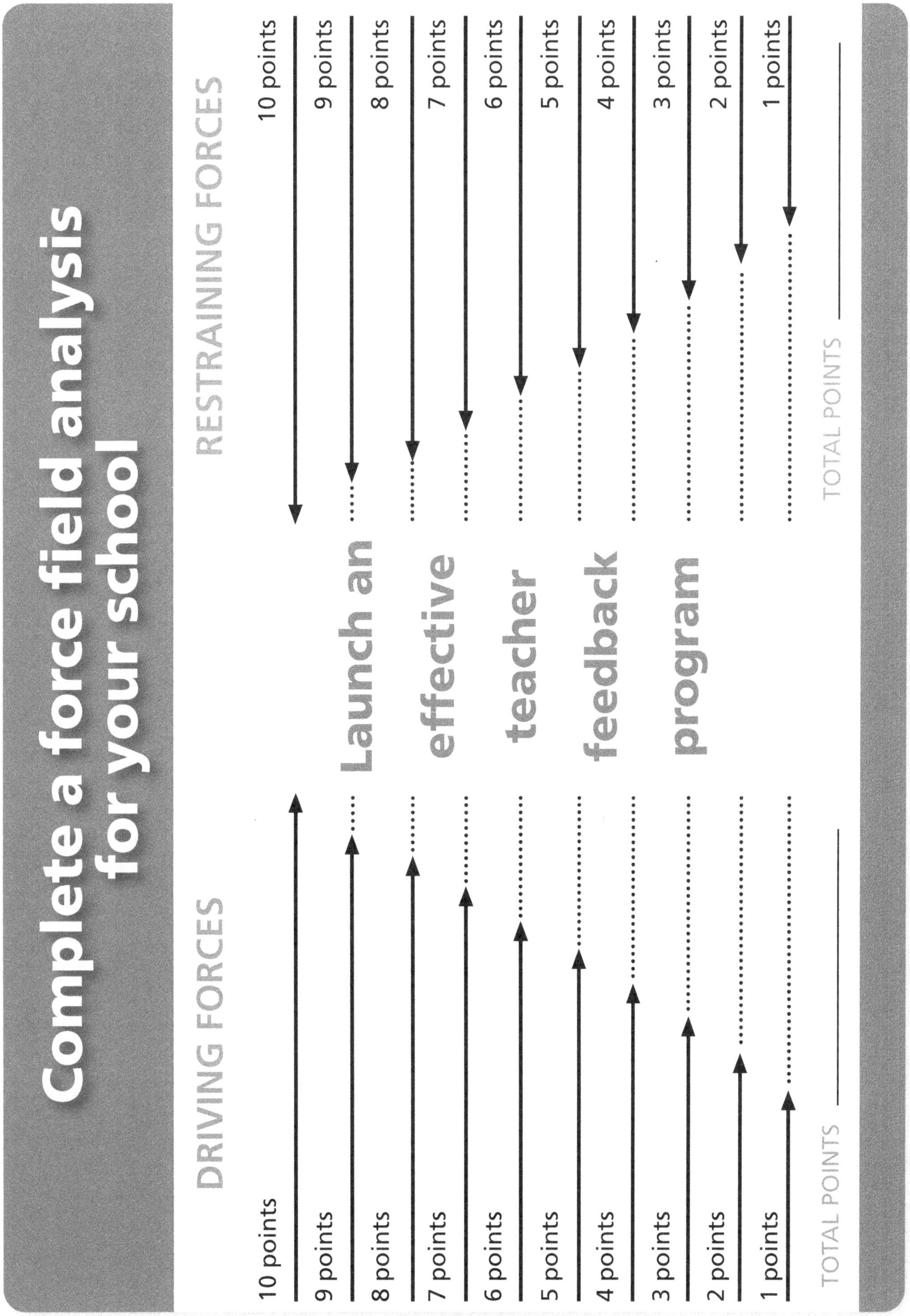

Step 6: Launch an effective teacher feedback program

Complete a force field analysis for your school

RESTRAINING FORCES

- 10 points
- 9 points
- 8 points
- 7 points
- 6 points
- 5 points
- 4 points
- 3 points
- 2 points
- 1 points

TOTAL POINTS _____

Launch an effective teacher feedback program

DRIVING FORCES

- 10 points
- 9 points
- 8 points
- 7 points
- 6 points
- 5 points
- 4 points
- 3 points
- 2 points
- 1 points

TOTAL POINTS _____

Figure 18   Adapted from Lewin (1943)

Step 7
Apply four strategies for providing effective feedback

At this stage in the Pirozzo Process, the observer has amassed the following knowledge and skills:

- an understanding of leadership styles
- time-management skills
- familiarity with curriculum planning
- expertise in using a variety of thinking tools
- conflict-resolution skills
- tools for the successful implementation of an effective teacher feedback program

Now, as the final step of the process, you will learn how to apply four different tools for providing constructive feedback:

- the former Sunshine Coast Region's coaching model form
- the unit evaluation form
- the classroom observation matrices
- the teacher feedback form

The coaching model

There are a variety of coaching terms and models, including team coaching, technical coaching, performance coaching, career coaching, skills coaching, cognitive coaching, challenge coaching and peer coaching. Each model is slightly different, but all have the same end goal, which is to improve the classroom practices that lead to improved student learning. For the purposes of this book, coaching refers to a process in which two or more teachers work together to

- improve teaching performance, leading to higher levels of student learning
- share professional knowledge and skills
- conduct classroom observation and evaluation
- provide feedback on one another's teaching practices

Why coaching matters

Traditionally, teachers have been expected to look after their own professional learning. I clearly remember my first teaching appointment, when the head of department kindly provided me with a box of white chalk and the list of my classes and told me to 'go and get them'. In fact, for the entire two years that I remained at this school, no professional development programs were offered to me. Can you imagine that happening to an athlete, a doctor or lawyer? This issue is taken up by Collins (2013):

> Most successful athletes would not consider working without a coach, professional singers would almost certainly have a voice coach, and even people wanting to improve their fitness more and more are turning to personal coaches. In the professions, lawyers are required to complete practical legal training under a more experienced legal professional before they are admitted, and doctors to complete an internship with an experienced medical professional before they receive general registration. In education, until recently, school-based coaching under the mentoring of an experienced professional has been the exception rather than the rule. (p. 1)

Over the years, I have discovered that my experiences were shared by many educators; in fact, receiving no coaching or mentoring support was common. Instead, schools have typically relied on sending their staff to 'one-shot' professional learning opportunities, such as one-day workshops and conferences.

But recently educators have begun to question the validity and effectiveness of this approach. According to Russo (2004),

> Many of the more conventional forms of professional development – such as conferences, lectures, and mass teacher-institute days – are unpopular with educators because they are often led by outside experts who tell teachers what to do, then they are never heard from again. (p. 2)

Furthermore, the workshops and conferences that comprise most traditional staff development methodologies don't provide sufficient time to promote meaningful change (Garet et al. 2001). Foltos (2010) reports that 'teachers often don't have the skills or knowledge needed to apply what they learn in these workshops and have no way to receive support or feedback when they do attempt to apply what they have learned' (p. 1).

If one-shot professional development programs such as seminars, workshops and conferences don't work, what do the experts have to say about the characteristics of an effective staff development program? Russo (2004) suggests that such a program

> must be on-going, deeply embedded in teachers' classroom work with children, specific to grade levels or academic content, and focused on research-based approaches. It also must help to open classroom doors and create more collaboration and sense of community among teachers in a school. (p. 2)

Research indicates that one way to meet these requirements is to implement a dedicated system of instructional coaching. Joyce and Showers (1996, 2002), whose results are summarised in Table 4, found that skilling by itself did not ensure transfer, as shown by the fact that only about 5 per cent of teachers implemented new ideas learned in traditional staff development settings. But when seminar participation was combined with coaching, 90 per cent of teachers were found to be using the newly learned strategies in their classrooms.

Mode of teaching	Skill attainment	Skill transfer
Theory (e.g. seminars)	5%	5%
Theory + demonstration (e.g. seminars)	10%	5%
Theory + demonstration + practice + feedback (e.g. seminars)	95%	5%
Theory + demonstration + practice + feedback + coaching (e.g in classrooms)	95%	90%

Table 4   Adapted with permission from Joyce and Showers (1996, 2002)

Moreover, in addition to its demonstrable impact on the efficacy of professional learning, coaching provides teachers with the opportunity to

- interact and collaborate with other teachers
- develop trust, leading to increased support
- become involved in meaningful discussion, planning, observation and reflection
- receive non-judgemental and non-evaluative feedback
- discuss concepts, skills and problems that may arise in their classrooms and within their areas of expertise
- implement different forms of differentiation
- experiment with a variety of thinking tools
- feel less isolated from their fellow teachers
- create a forum for addressing instructional problems
- develop an enhanced sense of professional skill
- gain an increased ability to analyse their own lessons
- explore new ideas, models and practices
- widen their repertoire of instructional strategies
- most importantly, improve their teaching performance, leading to higher levels of student achievement

It should be noted that while many educators malign the one-shot approach, I continue to be convinced that workshops, seminars and conferences are extremely cost-effective methods of disseminating and sharing new information, ideas, models and programs. As such, they should not be discarded but rather retained by schools as an integral part of their overall professional development programs. In support of this view, Joyce and Showers (1982) conclude that 'coaching without the study of theory, the observation of demonstration, and the opportunity for practice with feedback will, in fact accomplish very little' (p. 5).

How to implement a coaching program

Here is my 9-point approach for implementing a feedback program based on the coaching model:

1. Develop a pool of expert teachers in every school. These are teachers that have a very high level of credibility within their schools, are listened to by other teachers and have developed outstanding relationships with students, parents, teachers, administrators and members of the local community.

2. Have members of the administration and heads of department providing the observer and the teacher with the necessary release time so that no funds will be needed to hire outside coaches. For example, why not invite members of the administrative team to teach a class for one period a day thus enabling the teachers to participate in the coaching program? Alternatively, schools could enable both the observer and the teacher to participate in this program by releasing them from playground, bus or sporting duties. This approach worked extremely well in a large metropolitan high school where we ran a cluster program for gifted and talented students on Tuesday afternoon. Teachers who wanted to be involved in this program were released from participating in sports every Tuesday afternoon.

3. Organise team teaching thus providing teachers with more flexibility.

4. Bring a number of classes together for a specific subject area.

5. Involve teachers-aides.

6. Encourage in-service teachers to be involved.

7. Implement a vertical timetabling and unitisation program.

8. Offer integrated studies culminating in the completion of RATs.

9. Implement the Pirozzo Model for Differentiation so that teachers can specialise in offering a minimum of six effective learning and teaching strategies: ability grouping, cooperative learning teams, learning contracts, learning centres, multi-age grouping and individual learning plans (see Pirozzo 2014 for more information).

Having been involved in mentoring and feedback programs for a number of years, I firmly believe that it would be extremely beneficial to have an instructional coach in every school – or for that matter, one for every teacher. But my observation has been that many schools will only implement a coaching program if it doesn't drain the school's finances. Any such program has to cost very little to implement and maintain, or it will disappear as soon as the school, department of education or diocese encounters financial difficulties. It is for this reason that unlike most other feedback programs currently available, my process requires almost no financial investment by the school.

The 9-point process also has an advantage over other instructional feedback programs in that the individuals who take on the role of observer are already established members of the school community. The recruitment of coaches from outside the school has many potential downsides, from the problem of finding enough coaches in specialist subject areas to the inability of coaches to establish productive relationships with school-based staff due to their ignorance of the prevailing school culture.

Finding enough effective coaches can be a real problem particularly in areas such as mathematics and science. I recall with some trepidation the difficulties that I often faced as a former head of science in finding enough teachers to cover all the senior chemistry and physics classes let alone finding coaches in these areas.

Once found, schools must provide support for coaches to increase their own skills and there is a cost involved in hiring coaches and providing non-contact time for both the coach and the teacher being coached. Indeed, there is always the issue of cost if we decide to hire coaches from outside the school. For example, in 2003 the city of Boston alone spent 5.8 million dollars to support 75 coaches in 97 schools (Neufeld & Roper 2003).

In difficult financial times, the Pirozzo Process will have a greater chance of ongoing success than programs that rely on hiring coaches from outside the school. In addition, while observers and teachers will not receive any additional remuneration for their participation in this program, their involvement could become an integral part of the selection process for teachers seeking promotion. By following my guidelines, not only will schools save a huge amount of money, but they will also establish a coaching program that reflects the unique needs, aspirations and the culture of the school.

The SCR coaching model

Now we are ready to study in detail the coaching feedback program that was implemented within the former Sunshine Coast Region (SCR) in the early 1990s. As gifted and talented consultant within the SCR during this time, I participated in this region's observation and conferencing program, and I have been building upon what I learnt then ever since.

The following coaching model has been adapted from the material developed by the SCR (n.d.), with permission of the Queensland Department of Education, Training and Employment. As well as five types and four phases of feedback, it includes guidelines for constructive classroom observation. On page 58 is a copy of the SCR's coaching model form, which you may like to use to provide effective feedback to your teachers.

Five types of feedback

1. Observer identifies only what was effective and why it was effective, so that the teacher becomes aware of the good things that they are doing.
2. Observer and teacher identify what was effective and discuss what else might work. They generate alternative teaching and learning strategies by answering the question, 'If you could do this lesson again, what would you do differently?'
3. Teacher identifies an area of concern, then observer and teacher brainstorm alternative teaching and learning strategies.

Implementing an Effective Teacher Feedback Program

SCR coaching model form

Observer	
Teacher	
Date	
Unit	
Year	

As you observe the lesson, write down what the teacher says and the students' responses (in their exact words, not your interpretations).

Figure 19   Adapted with permission from SCR (n.d.)

Step 7: Apply four strategies for providing effective feedback

4. Observer identifies an area of concern that is not evident to the teacher. Observer assists the teacher to develop alternative teaching and learning strategies.

5. Teacher is now ready to help others by modelling and observing their lessons. In other words, the teacher becomes the observer. The aim is to promote ongoing professional growth and development.

Note that even though types 1, 2 and 3 require no negative feedback, they offer tremendous potential for professional growth because the teacher is required to reflect on what is working in their classroom and consider alternative strategies.

Four phases of feedback

1. Pre-observation

    The teacher and the observer enter into a mutually satisfactory agreement about the structure process. The teacher makes two key choices:

    - What will be observed?
    - What type of feedback will be provided (1, 2, 3, 4 or 5)?

2. Observation

    The lesson chosen by the teacher is observed, and the observer records specific details of the lesson. The observer reports only on what was agreed.

3. Feedback

    The observer provides the teacher with feedback by asking two questions:

    - What did you like about the lesson and why?
    - If you were to teach a similar lesson again, what would you do differently?

4. Post-observation

    Once feedback has been provided, the observer asks the teacher:

    - What have you learned from this feedback?
    - What should we move on to next?

SCR guidelines for observation

Below are SCR's guidelines for observation and feedback. The guidelines are designed to help the observer gather relevant data and provide effective feedback to the teacher.

1. Teacher selects what is to be observed. The agenda is controlled by the teacher – no surprises.

2. Teacher selects class and time.

3. Observer collects data that
    a. is specific
    b. uses the exact words used by the teacher and the students

3. Find a private, comfortable, quiet spot and spend 20–30 minutes providing feedback.

4. Observer asks, 'What did you like about your lesson?'
    a. Allow time to reflect.
    b. Focus on the lesson and what worked.
    c. Encourage the teacher to begin to analyse the lesson.

5. Observer asks, 'Is there anything that you would do differently?'
    a. Empower the teacher by identifying unsatisfactory areas and asking them to propose different strategies.
    b. Focus on things that can be improved rather than on problems.
    c. Avoid 'I would' and 'You should', as these statements can trigger resentment

6. Observer goes through the data gathered during the classroom visits and shares their actual observations (not interpretations) with the teacher. Student responses to situations may now be discussed.

7. Teacher and observer work together to develop a collegiate problem-solving approach to classroom situations and brainstorm alternatives.

8. Observer concludes the discussion by asking the teacher, 'What is your major learning from today?'

9. Observer shares their major learning from observing the teacher. Sharing of learnings develops trust as it shows that observation is a two-way process.

10. Observer and teacher agree on future observations with special attention to what lesson to observe next, time and place.

Providing effective feedback using non-coaching strategies

The coaching model is extremely valuable, but it does take a good deal of time and effort to implement and monitor. As a result, there are circumstances in which the coaching model alone will not do. In addition to the coaching model, I have devised three additional tools for providing effective feedback to teachers. The tools are described below, along with a scenario to help teachers understand the appropriate time to use each one.

Unit evaluation form

On pages 61–62, you will find a copy of our unit evaluation form. In order to provide effective feedback to teachers on their unit planning, it will be essential that both the observer and the teacher also have access to the following items:

- 10 points to follow in order to create outstanding units (page 22)
- the Learning and Teaching Wheel (page 20)
- the Engaging Wheel (page 21)
- the Australian Curriculum

Step 7: Apply four strategies for providing effective feedback

Unit evaluation form

Observer	Teacher	Date	Unit	Year

Criteria	Yes	No	Amendments	Resubmit date
1. Have content descriptions from the Australian Curriculum been selected as a basis for the unit?				
2. a. Have the RATs been created, placed in the HOTS area of the Pirozzo Matrix and coloured in yellow? b. Has a rubric been created for each RAT?				
3. How many of Gardner's eight multiple intelligences has the teacher provided for using the Engaging Wheel?				
4. Have critical verbs and related project types been selected by the teacher for each level of Bloom's taxonomy using the Learning and Teaching Wheel?				

Table 5 (1 of 2)

Criteria	Yes	No	Amendments	Resubmit date
5. Has the teacher decided which learning activities they will teach explicitly, and have these activities been coloured in blue on the matrix?				
6. Has the teacher decided which choices they will provide to the students, and have the choice activities been left in white on the matrix?				
7. Has the teacher devised a number of cooperative learning activities using the Pirozzo Matrix?				
8. Have a minimum of five thinking tools been included to help students engage with the unit?				
9. Has the teacher numbered their activities on the Pirozzo Matrix to show the sequence in which they will be teaching the unit?				
10. Has the teacher provided a comprehensive list of the resources needed to teach the unit?				

Table 5 (2 of 2)

Step 7: Apply four strategies for providing effective feedback

Scenario

You are one of the school leaders at a large primary school that employs 85 teachers. As part of your duties, you are expected to certify that teachers' units are properly prepared – which means that they have depth, rigour, engagement and require students to use LOTS, HOTS and a variety of thinking tools in order to create RATs.

Normally, it takes you about two hours to read, interpret and provide effective feedback on a single teacher's unit. In your current role, you have 85 units to assess and provide feedback, but it is unlikely that you will be able to find 170 hours to spend on observing and providing feedback.

The good news is that my unit evaluation form enables you to provide effective and efficient feedback to each teacher in about 10–15 minutes. As a bonus, the form is very easy to interpret, and your teachers know exactly what they need to do to get their units accredited.

Classroom observation matrix

This version of the Pirozzo Matrix (see p. 64) is designed for the observer to use when visiting the teacher in their classroom. It will enable you to

- get a quick snapshot of what is happening in this classroom by recording what the teacher and the students are saying on either the 48- or the 56-grid classroom observation matrix
- register exactly what is taking place in terms of the range of questions being asked (LOTS and HOTS) and the learning styles being addressed
- see the range of thinking tools being used
- discover what differentiation strategies are being implemented
- provide effective feedback based on what is actually taking place in this classroom rather than relying on other people's comments

The following scenario is based on a real experience of mine, but names have been changed so as not to offend anyone.

Scenario

You are the head of teaching and learning at a large high school. The majority of the teachers have taught at the school for a very long time, and many will retire within the next five years. On a regular basis, you are receiving complaints about one veteran teacher in particular. Other teachers approach you because the noise level emanating from Mr Tearwood's classroom is intolerable, while parents are adamant that unless something is done they will move their children to other neighbouring schools.

The administrative team is aware of these complaints and have scheduled a meeting for the following Friday. Given the short period of time available, you realise that you need to visit Mr Tearwood's classroom to gather your own data rather than relying on hearsay.

48-grid classroom observation matrix

Observer: Teacher: Date: Unit: Subject: Year:

Multiple intelligences	Bloom's taxonomy					
	KNOWING	UNDERSTANDING	APPLYING	ANALYSING	CREATING	EVALUATING
VERBAL — I enjoy reading, writing and speaking.						
MATHEMATICAL — I enjoy working with numbers and science.						
VISUAL/SPATIAL — I enjoy painting, drawing and visualising.						
KINESTHETIC — I enjoy doing hands-on activities, sports and dance.						
MUSICAL — I enjoy making and listening to music.						
INTERPERSONAL — I enjoy working with others.						
INTRAPERSONAL — I enjoy working by myself.						
NATURALIST — I enjoy caring for plants and animals.						

Figure 20   Adapted from Pirozzo (2007)

56-grid classroom observation matrix

Observer: Teacher: Date: Unit: Subject: Year:

Multiple intelligences	Bloom's taxonomy						
	PRE-KNOWING	KNOWING	UNDERSTANDING	APPLYING	ANALYSING	CREATING	EVALUATING
VERBAL — I enjoy reading, writing and speaking.							
MATHEMATICAL — I enjoy working with numbers and science.							
VISUAL/SPATIAL — I enjoy painting, drawing and visualising.							
KINESTHETIC — I enjoy doing hands-on activities, sports and dance.							
MUSICAL — I enjoy making and listening to music.							
INTERPERSONAL — I enjoy working with others.							
INTRAPERSONAL — I enjoy working by myself.							
NATURALIST — I enjoy caring for plants and animals.							

Figure 21   Adapted from Pirozzo (2007)

Step 7: Apply four strategies for providing effective feedback

48-grid classroom observation matrix

Observer: You **Teacher:** Mr Tearwood **Date:** 09/09/15 **Unit:** The human body **Subject:** Science **Year:** 6

Multiple intelligences	Bloom's taxonomy					
	KNOWING	UNDERSTANDING	APPLYING	ANALYSING	CREATING	EVALUATING
VERBAL — I enjoy reading, writing and speaking.	Make notes on the human body.	Summarise how the human body works.	Write a report on an illness of your choice.			
MATHEMATICAL — I enjoy working with numbers and science.	Complete heartbeat activity sheets.	Find some statistics about your body.	Make a graph ordering the parts of the body from smallest to largest.			
VISUAL/SPATIAL — I enjoy painting, drawing and visualising.	Compare two types of joints.	Draw these two joints.	Write a 200-word report on how joints work.			
KINESTHETIC — I enjoy doing hands-on activities, sports and dance.	What are muscles? Write a definition.	What is the function of muscles? Explain.	Prepare a five-minute talk explaining how you feel when your muscles get tired.			
MUSICAL — I enjoy making and listening to music.	Copy notes on how music relaxes the body.	Find five songs that have a 'body systems' theme.	Write a two-verse rap about your body.			
INTERPERSONAL — I enjoy working with others.	What does it mean to stay healthy?	List the types of foods that we should eat to stay healthy.	Write about how you keep your body healthy.			
INTRAPERSONAL — I enjoy working by myself.	Explain to your group, how you keep your body healthy.	Copy notes on healthy foods.	Write a letter to the editor explaining how you feel when you see fast foods being advertised.			
NATURALIST — I enjoy caring for plants and animals.	What are herbs?	How do we grow herbs?	Write about how herbs help us to stay healthy.			

Figure 22   Adapted from Pirozzo (2007)

Mr Tearwood agrees that you can visit his classroom on 10 different occasions, as long as the union representative is present. He requests that you visit during science lessons, which take place early in the morning and last about 40 minutes. Apparently, science is one of this teacher's areas of expertise; the classroom is well equipped with plenty of basic science equipment, and there is a separate area for the teacher to carry out science experiments.

You observe Mr Tearwood teaching the children for 10 days. The results of your observations are summarised on page 65. By comparing the activities that this teacher has planned with the 10 steps for creating outstanding units (see p. 22), you notice that this unit doesn't contain any

- RATs or rubrics
- higher-order thinking activities – it's all lower-order thinking
- choices – it's all teacher's talk
- differentiation strategies – the teacher is doing all the work
- thinking tools – none to be seen

When asked about his approach to unit planning, Mr Tearwood replies, 'Give me a break! I've been teaching this unit for so long that I could do it in my sleep. Anyway, why write anything down when you have mastered the subject area?'

Reflection

Based on the observations on page 65, what do you suggest that the head of teaching and learning should do next?

_____
_____
_____
_____
_____

Teacher feedback form

Scenario

You are the principal of a large rural school in a very isolated area. Because of the school's location, most of the staff appointed are first-year teachers who will stay for a maximum of two years and then move closer to the state's capital city.

In this state, first-year teachers are granted provisional status. Once they have taught for at least 200 days, they can apply for full registration. To accompany the application, the principal has to complete a full registration recommendation report. To assist you in getting your teachers ready for accreditation, the teacher feedback form (pp. 67–74) has been designed. The principal should visit each first-year teacher's classroom a number of times, and each visit should focus on a different phase of the teacher's progress.

Step 7: Apply four strategies for providing effective feedback

Teacher feedback form

Observer	Teacher	Date	Unit	Year

Phase 1: Getting the classroom ready

	Yes	No	N/A	Comments
Provides the students with a safe working environment (e.g. ensures that extension cords and powerboards are taped to the floor, the fish tank is placed on top of a solid table located at the corner of the room).				
Views films, videos, YouTube to ensure that the material covered is appropriate for the students' age.				
Checks that the equipment to be used is in proper working order (e.g. Bunsen burners, ovens).				

Table 6 (1 of 8)

Phase 2: Welcoming the students

	Yes	No	N/A	Comments
Welcomes students by using positive comments, eye contact, smiling and addressing them by their first names.				
Guides the students to enter the classroom smoothly and quietly.				
Settles students quickly.				
Ensures that the noise level is low.				

Step 7: Apply four strategies for providing effective feedback

Phase 3: Introducing today's lesson

	Yes	No	N/A	Comments
Uses a variety of 'hooks' to activate students' interest (e.g. writes a specific word on the board or a quote to stimulate their curiosity) (e.g. Infinity).				
Reviews material covered in the previous lesson(s).				
Checks for prior learning.				
Clearly identifies the RATs that the students will be able to create by the end of the lesson and/or unit. The RATs are shaded in Yellow.				
Sets clear expectations relating to the quality of RATs by providing the students with relevant rubrics. Rubrics will be used for teaching, assessment and reporting purposes.				

	Yes	No	N/A	Comments
Shares with students how they will be guided and assisted in completing their RATs. In other words, the students will know exactly how they are going to get there.				
Introduces new material in an exciting and engaging manner.				

Phase 4: Delivering the lesson

	Yes	No	N/A	Comments
Uses a variety of seating arrangements (e.g. lecture style, cooperative groups).				
Introduces and explains new words (e.g. photosynthesis) and builds a word and a spelling bank.				

Step 7: Apply four strategies for providing effective feedback

	Yes	No	N/A	Comments
Inspires the students by using a variety of thinking tools (e.g. LDC, LITE, LEADER).				
Facilitates the acquisition of knowledge by asking students to research certain topics and then to share what they have learnt with other children using TPS/TPSS.				
In delivering the explicit teaching activities (shaded in blue on the matrix), the teacher engages the students with learning that has depth and rigour rather than fluff.				
Caters for students' different learning styles.				
Provides students with choices (shaded in black and white on the matrix).				

	Yes	No	N/A	Comments
Differentiates the curriculum by using a variety of effective learning and teaching strategies (e.g. ability grouping, cooperative learning teams, learning contracts, learning centres, multi-age grouping, individual learning plans).				
Employs lower order thinking skills questions (LOTS).				
Employs higher order thinking skills questions (HOTS).				
Uses humour whenever appropriate.				
Paces the lesson well.				

Step 7: Apply four strategies for providing effective feedback

	Yes	No	N/A	Comments
Regularly checks with the students to ensure that they understand the material covered by asking probing questions (e.g. 'What would happen if …').				
Relies on various technologies to make the lesson exciting and relevant (e.g. IWB, YouTube).				
Provides appropriate praises.				
Deals with any form of discipline and/or bullying in a decisive and efficient manner with due regard to students' self esteem.				

Phase 5: Finishing the lesson

	Yes	No	N/A	Comments
Checks to make sure that the students have learnt the critical material taught by asking them pertinent questions (e.g. What factors impact on global warming?).				
Collects work to be marked and assessed.				
Assigns work that the students can complete at home (e.g. solving a number of maths problems, viewing a particular television program, getting ready for a debate).				
Dismisses the class in an orderly and positive manner.				

Step 7: Apply four strategies for providing effective feedback

	Yes	No	N/A	Comments
Regularly checks with the students to ensure that they understand the material covered by asking probing questions (e.g. 'What would happen if …').				
Relies on various technologies to make the lesson exciting and relevant (e.g. IWB, YouTube).				
Provides appropriate praises.				
Deals with any form of discipline and/or bullying in a decisive and efficient manner with due regard to students' self esteem.				

Implementing an Effective Teacher Feedback Program

Phase 5: Finishing the lesson

	Yes	No	N/A	Comments
Checks to make sure that the students have learnt the critical material taught by asking them pertinent questions (e.g. What factors impact on global warming?).				
Collects work to be marked and assessed.				
Assigns work that the students can complete at home (e.g. solving a number of maths problems, viewing a particular television program, getting ready for a debate).				
Dismisses the class in an orderly and positive manner.				

Step 7: Apply four strategies for providing effective feedback

Reflection

Once you have studied the report and thought about how you might use it, try to answer the following questions.

Will this form assist you in getting your first-year teachers ready for full registration?

_____
_____
_____
_____
_____

What changes, omissions or additions should be made to this form in order to improve it?

_____
_____
_____
_____
_____

In addition to using this form with your first-year teachers, could you also use it to provide effective feedback to teachers who have been on leave for a number of years and have decided to return to teaching?

_____
_____
_____
_____
_____

Could you also use it to support teachers who are getting ready for promotion? If yes, what additional information should be added to this form?

_____
_____
_____
_____
_____

Reflection

References

Ayazit, M & Mannix, EA 2003, 'Should I stay or should I go? Predicting team members' intent to remain in the team', *Small Group Research*, vol. 34, no. 3, pp. 290–321.

Bloom, BS (ed.) 1984 (1956), *Taxonomy of educational objectives: Handbook I, Cognitive domain*, 2nd edn, Longman, New York, USA.

Bruner, JS 1966, *Toward a theory of instruction*, Harvard University Press, Cambridge, USA.

Clarke, R 1999, 'A primer in diffusion of innovations theory', http://www.rogerclarke.com/SOS/InnDiff.html

Collins, R 2013, 'Research feature: School-based coaching', *Independent Schools Queensland: Briefings*, vol. 17, no. 3, pp. 1, 3–8.

Covey, SR 2013 (1989), *The 7 habits of highly effective people: Powerful lessons in personal change*, rev. edn, Simon & Schuster, New York, USA.

Culbertson, H 2014, 'Improving group, organizational or team dynamics when conflict occurs', Southern Nazarene University, http://home.snu.edu/~hculbert/conflict.htm

Drucker, PF 2006 (1967), *The effective executive: The definitive guide to getting the right things done*, rev. edn, Harper Business, New York, USA.

Foltos, L 2010, 'Peer coaching: Changing classroom practice and enhancing student achievement', http://www.edlabgroup.org/sites/default/files/documents/peercoachinglf.pdf

Forsyth, DR 2013, *Group dynamics*, 6th edn, Wadsworth Cengage Learning, Belmont, USA.

Fullan, M 2008, *The six secrets of change: What the best leaders do to help their organisations survive and thrive*, Jossey-Bass, San Francisco, USA.

Gardner, H 1999, *Intelligences reframed: Multiple intelligences for the 21st century*, Basic Books, New York, USA.

Gardner, H 2011 (1983), *Frames of mind: The theory of multiple intelligences*, rev. edn, Basic Books, New York, USA.

Garet, M, Porter, A, Desimone, L, Birman, B & Yoon, S 2001, 'What makes professional development effective? Results from a national sample of teachers', *American Educational Research Journal*, vol. 38, no. 4, pp. 915–945.

Glasser, W 1986, *Control theory in the classroom*, Harper & Row, New York, USA.

Goldfien, H & Robbennolt, JK 2007, 'What if the lawyers have their way? An empirical assessment of conflict strategies and attitudes toward mediation styles', *Ohio State Journal on Dispute Resolution*, vol. 22, pp. 277–320.

Hunt, H 2012, '8 steps to conflict resolution', *Training Daily Advisor*, http://trainingdailyadvisor.blr.com/2012/08/eight-steps-to-conflict-resolution

Joyce, B & Showers, B 2002 (1988), *Student achievement through staff development*, 3rd edn, Association for Supervision and Curriculum Development, Alexandria, USA.

Joyce, B & Showers, B 1982, 'The coaching of teaching', *Educational Leadership*, vol. 39, no. 1, pp. 4–10.

Joyce, B & Showers, B 1996, 'The evolution of peer coaching', *Educational Leadership*, vol. 53, no. 6, pp. 12–16.

Lewin, K 1943, Defining the 'field at a given time', *Psychological Review*, vol. 50, pp. 292–310.

Lewin, K, Lippit, R & White, RK 1939, 'Patterns of aggressive behaviour in experimentally created "social climates"', *Journal of Social Psychology*, vol 10, no. 2, pp. 269–299.

McTighe, J & Wiggins G 2005, *Understanding by Design*, 2nd edn, Hawker Brownlow Education, Melbourne.

Morrell, M & Capparell, S 2003, *Shackleton's way*, Nicholas Brealey Publishing, London, UK.

Neufeld, B & Roper, D 2003, *Coaching: A strategy for developing instructional capacity – Promises and practicalities*, Aspen Institute Program on Education & Annenberg Institute for School Reform, http://annenberginstitute.org/pdf/Coaching.pdf

Pirozzo, R 2024 (2006), *50 Cooperative Learning Activities: Engaging Thinking in Every Classroom*, 2nd edn, Amba Press, Melbourne.

Pirozzo, R 2024 (2014), *Differentiating the Curriculum: Supporting Teachers to Thrive in Mixed-ability Classrooms*, 2nd edn, Amba Press, Melbourne.

Pirozzo, R 2024 (2005, 2007), *Improving Thinking in the Classroom: Creating an Engaging, Exciting and Challenging Learning Environment*, 3rd edn, Amba Press, Melbourne.

Pirozzo, R 2024 (2013), *The Thinking School: Implementing Thinking Skills Across the School*, 2nd edn, Amba Press, Melbourne.

SCR (former Sunshine Coast Region) n.d., *Coaching*, Queensland Department of Education, Training and Employment, in possession of the author, Brisbane.

Rogers, EM 2003 (1962), *Diffusion of innovations*, 5th edn, Free Press, New York, USA.

Russo, A 2004, 'School-based coaching: A revolution in professional development – or just the latest fad?' *Harvard Education Letter*, vol. 20, no. 4, pp. 1–3.

Thomas, KW & Kilmann, RH 2015, 'An overview of the Thomas-Kilmann Conflict Mode Instrument (TKI)', http://www.kilmanndiagnostics.com/overview-thomas-kilmann-conflict-mode-instrument-tki

Van de Vliert, E & Euwema, MC 1994, 'Agreeableness and activeness as components of conflict behaviors', *Journal of Personality and Social Psychology*, vol. 66, no. 4, pp. 674–687.

Weeks, D 1992, *The eight essential steps to conflict resolution*, JP Tarcher, Los Angeles, USA.

Acknowledgements

I am grateful to the following individuals and publishers, whose work is excerpted in this book:

- *The 7 habits of highly effective people: Powerful lessons in personal change* by SR Covey, published by Simon & Schuster, 2013, excerpted with the permission of FranklinCovey.
- 'Coaching' by the SCR (former Sunshine Coast Region), excerpted with the permission of the Queensland Department of Education, Training and Employment.
- 'The coaching of teaching' by B Joyce and B Showers, published in *Educational Leadership* by the Association for Supervision and Curriculum Development, 1982, excerpted with the permission of the authors.
- *Diffusion of innovations* by EM Rogers, published by Free Press, 2003, excerpted with the permission of Simon & Schuster.
- *The effective executive: The definitive guide to getting the right things done* by PF Drucker, published by Harper Business, 2006, excerpted with the permission of the Peter F Drucker 1996 Literary Works Trust.
- 'Improving group, organizational or team dynamics when conflict occurs' by H Culbertson, 2014, available at http://home.snu.edu/~hculbert/conflict.htm, excerpted with the permission of the author.
- 'An overview of the Thomas-Kilmann Conflict Mode Instrument (TKI)' by KW Thomas and RH Kilmann, 2015, available at http://www.kilmanndiagnostics.com/overview-thomas-kilmann-conflict-mode-instrument-tki, excerpted with the permission of CPP.
- 'Patterns of aggressive behaviour in experimentally created "social climates"' by K Lewin, R Uppit and RK White, published in the *Journal of Social Psychology* by Taylor & Francis, 1939, excerpted with the permission of the publisher.
- *Shackleton's way* by M Morrell and S Capparell, published by Nicholas Brealey Publishing, 2003, excerpted with the permission of the publisher.
- *The six secrets of change: What the best leaders do to help their organisations survive and thrive* by M Fullan, published by Jossey-Bass, 2003, excerpted with the permission of the author.